ARCHIMEDES

Each book in the series GREAT LIVES IN THE ANCIENT WORLD succinctly explores the life, culture and lasting legacy of outstanding figures across the ancient world, including China, the Indian subcontinent, the Middle East, and ancient Greece and Rome.

SERIES EDITOR: Paul Cartledge

Archimedes: Fulcrum of Science   NICHOLAS NICASTRO
Plato: A Civic Life   CAROL ATACK

ARCHIMEDES

Fulcrum of Science

NICHOLAS NICASTRO

REAKTION BOOKS

To Barbara Finlay, with respect and appreciation

Published by
REAKTION BOOKS LTD
Unit 32, Waterside
44–48 Wharf Road
London N1 7UX, UK
www.reaktionbooks.co.uk

First published 2024
Copyright © Nicholas Nicastro 2024

Printed and bound in Great Britain by Bell & Bain, Glasgow

A catalogue record for this book is available from the British Library

ISBN 978 1 78914 922 7

CONTENTS

Note

THIS BOOK is intended to be a concise introduction to the life and legacy of Archimedes of Syracuse. It is designed for the lay reader and is essentially descriptive. Though it surveys key features of his thought, it is not meant to provide a comprehensive recitation of his mathematics, but instead to give a sense of its significance and flavour. Readers interested in the more exhaustive description (for example, to be walked through the exact steps of his proofs) are referred to the Suggested Reading for further study, particularly the works of Thomas Heath, Wilbur R. Knorr and Reviel Netz.

In accordance with current academic practice, ancient (BC) and modern (AD) eras are referred to here as BCE (Before the Common Era) and CE (Common Era), unless directly quoted with the old acronyms.

Chronology

1258	House of Wisdom destroyed in Baghdad
1269	William of Moerbeke publishes Latin translation of Archimedes' works
1586	Galileo publishes *La bilancetta*
c. 1740	Buffon 'recreates' burning mirrors of Archimedes
1851	Mariette excavates the Circle of Philosophers and Poets at Saqqara
1901	Antikythera Mechanism recovered
1910	Johan Heiberg publishes works from Archimedes Palimpsest

1 Giuseppe Nogari, *Archimedes*, 18th century, oil on canvas.

Prologue

'How inferior are all other minds compared with Archimedes,' declared Galileo. Carl Friedrich Gauss crowned him the first 'epoch-making mathematician'. Nikola Tesla called him 'my ideal'. Leonardo da Vinci and Newton acknowledged him as their antecedent and their inspiration. That Archimedes merited praise from such disparate geniuses testifies to the breadth and magnitude of what he achieved. Alfred North Whitehead asserted, 'in the year 1500 Europe knew less than Archimedes who died in the year 212 BC.' If history is increasingly an account of the transformation of human experience by the fruits of scientific rationalism, then Archimedes is one of the most consequential persons who ever lived.

He casts a long shadow, but the man himself has long been draped in darkness. Though we pretty well know the year of his death (212 BCE), his birth year of 287 BCE is only a matter of inference, based on a statement by a Byzantine historian living more than a thousand years later. We have no verified likenesses in any medium. There was a biography of him by a contemporary named Heracleides, but it is lost. Much of what we know about the details of his life is therefore sketchy, secondary or simply invented.

The indistinctness of Archimedes as a person has long thwarted historians, but has also served to magnify his legend, as if his accomplishments were handed down from a demigod who never grew up, loved anyone or needed to scratch himself. There is one detail about him that is charming (if, alas, late): Archimedes was so preoccupied with his studies that he neglected his physical person. 'When he was dragged by main force, as he often was, to the place for bathing and anointing his body,' wrote the Roman-era Greek biographer Plutarch, 'he would trace geometrical figures in the ashes, and draw lines with his finger in the oil with which his body was anointed, being possessed by a great delight, and in very truth a captive of the Muses.'[1]

We do not know if Archimedes had a sense of humour, but he may have been amused by the fact that, in the early years of the third millennium CE, he is now having something of a moment. New technology has made possible the recovery of entire lost works from parchment that was recycled as a prayer book in the thirteenth century. This so-called 'Archimedes Palimpsest' has elevated appreciation of his work in pioneering the concepts that underlay integral calculus and, in turn, many of the technologies that define modernity.[2] Meanwhile, updated analyses of inscriptions on the Antikythera Mechanism, an ancient analogue computer recovered from the sea in 1901, may date the device possibly close to the lifetime of Archimedes himself. All of this has contributed to a re-evaluation of the magnitude of scientific and technological sophistication reached in antiquity – as well as debates over why the Babylonians, Egyptians, Greeks and Romans did not progress further than they did.

In his trains of scrupulously grounded inferences, his insistence on quantitative rigour, his immunity from moral or metaphysical presumptions, Archimedes is the first figure in history to sound like a fully modern scientist. Should any more of his lost treatises be found, it is a veritable certainty that such quaint beliefs as 'planets move in circles because the circle is the most perfect shape' or 'objects fall to earth because they seek their proper place' will not be found in them. Giants like Leonardo, Galileo and Tesla gazed across the millennia and recognized in him – and not in Aristotle, nor such notables as Galen or Ptolemy – their archetype. Archimedes embodied what science would become at its most powerful, thousands of years before that potential began to be realized.

1

Engineer

Marcus Tullius Cicero was a politician on the rise in the year 75 BCE. At 31 years old, he had begun his ascent of the *cursus honorum*, the ladder of Roman civic magistracies, when he became quaestor in western Sicily. The job was largely one of balancing the government's books. Involving as it did no command of military forces, it was hardly the kind of position that garnered much political power in late Republican Rome. But Cicero made it serve him in several important ways.

First, he performed his duties with exceptional competence. This was hardly what the natives had learned to expect from their Roman overlords, who more often approached duty on the island as a kind of smash-and-grab job. For his integrity, he earned such gratitude from the Sicilians that they hired Cicero to prosecute Gaius Verres, a Roman governor whose rapacity was truly legendary.

Verres' exploits included skimming the cream from confiscatory taxes, brazen looting of temples and private homes, and an ongoing project to acquire the most beautiful of local wives and daughters for his personal enjoyment. So thoroughly did he enrich himself that by the end of his term what was once Rome's bread-basket teetered on the edge of famine. Cicero, an orator of great skill, won his prosecution of Verres, defeating his older rival Quintus Hortensius Hortalus. He was well on his way to becoming consul in 63 BCE, at the youngest legal age for that high post, and was one of the key protagonists in the drama that ultimately led to the dissolution of the Roman Republic.

More relevant here is an incident Cicero reports in his *Tusculan Disputations*.[1] Though his quaestorship in Sicily was based in Lilybaeum in the west of the island, his Hellenophilia led him to the still-resplendent city of Syracuse on the east coast. There he took it upon himself (he does not explain why) to discover the final resting place of a 'humble and obscure mathematician of the same city, called Archimedes'. The locals were no help in this quest – 'the Syracusans knew nothing of it'. Cicero, armed only with his determination and self-professed erudition, went looking anyway. After leading a deputation of city officials outside the city walls on what they probably considered a wild goose chase, Cicero discovered an overgrown tomb topped by a sculpture of a sphere enclosed in a cylinder, a key detail he remembered from some literary source he doesn't name (possibly the biography by Heracleides). Tools were fetched to clear the weeds from the neglected monument, and lo, there were the verses he expected to see. 'Thus one of the noblest cities of Greece,' boasts Cicero, 'and one which at one time likewise had been very celebrated for learning, had known nothing of the monument of its greatest genius, if it had not been discovered to them by a native of Arpinum.'

Cicero has his own purpose in telling this story. The overarching theme of the *Disputations* is the nature of true happiness: does it lie in power, fame or riches, or in the more profound virtues of wisdom, patience, love of country? In Cicero's telling, Archimedes was somehow both Greece's 'greatest genius', yet also 'obscure', his ashes lying in a forgotten grave. It is tempting to think Cicero exaggerates the ignorance of the Syracusans to aggrandize himself – the provincial shit-kicker from Arpinum who is destined for immortality just as surely as he physically gravitates towards the greatness of Archimedes. Like many a colonialist scholar of later centuries, he exhibits his fitness to rule by teaching the ignorant natives about their own history.

Whatever his motives, Cicero restored Archimedes' grave. He remains our sole literary witness to the final resting place of one of history's greatest minds, confirming at least elements of the accounts of Polybius, Livy and Plutarch. And his discovery inspired a small school of painters, as Francesco Zuccarelli (Italy, 1702–1788), Martin Knoller (Austrian, 1725–1804), Benjamin West (American/British, 1738–1820) and Pierre-Henri de Valenciennes (France, 1750–1819) all envisioned the moment when, sickle in hand, Cicero salvaged genius from oblivion. Their treatments vary a bit in certain details, such as whether they depict the sphere and cylinder on the grave, as well as in approach, from Rococo to academic-historical to *plein air* landscape. They are united,

2 Francesco Zuccarelli, *Cicero Discovering the Grave of Archimedes*, 1747, oil on canvas.

however, in being near-contemporaries: they could easily have gathered in a parlour for drinks anytime before Zuccarelli's death in 1788. Their treatments share a cautionary edge, a reminder that even the greatest things are subject to the whims of time, the great leveller. Their pathos implies – in fact, depends upon – a certain identification with the 'lost' Archimedes, a sense that the advances of what would become called the European Enlightenment could just as easily end up hidden under brambles.

Cicero preserved Archimedes' physical memorial, but only temporarily. Under the assaults of centuries of Verres' successors, the tomb was lost again. The city of Syracuse, battered and pauperized, retreated back to its original limits on the island of Ortygia. Equally damaging was the rebound in recent times, when the city grew explosively over its former territories on the mainland. If that sphere and cylinder ever saw the light of day again, they were likely not seen by anyone as versed in antiquities as Cicero.

Instead, modern Syracuse honours her greatest figure by calling a Roman grave – centuries too young, in the wrong style and in the wrong place – the 'Tomb of Archimedes'. If we go to the northeast corner of the Neapolis Archaeological Park now, we find a sign that simultaneously extols the structure as such, but then corrects itself that it is definitely *not* the tomb.

Could it be that as early as Cicero's quaestorship, a mere 137 years after his death, and in his home town, aspects of Archimedes' life had already lapsed into legend? It is a question we will have occasion to ponder as we trace his legacy through the centuries. We will also return to the specific question of his final resting place. For now, we turn to what is known and what is lost about the living man. Who was this person who knew more than anyone alive in Europe over the next 2,000 years?

Geometry of a Life

'Archimedes, that machinist, was a Syracusan by race, an old geometrician, [who drove] past seventy-five seasons.'[2] Thus writes the twelfth-century CE Byzantine historian John Tzetzes, placing Archimedes' birth at around 287 BCE (having died in 212 BCE after 75 'seasons'). Based on correction of a few mangled words in the introduction to his *Sand-Reckoner*, we know his father's name was Phidias, and he was an astronomer. Archimedes' family appears to have been of long lineage in Syracuse: again according to Tzetzes, the Romans buried Archimedes' remains in his ancestral tomb, suggesting his family had a generational presence in the city.[3] Curiously, Plutarch also calls Archimedes a 'kinsman' of King Hieron II of Syracuse (308–215 BCE). Hieron himself was the bastard son of Hierocles, who claimed to be descended from the tyrant Gelon.[4] Archimedes' 'kinship' with Hieron is therefore hard to interpret – was he most associated with the king's humble, maternal side, or was Archimedes also related to Hierocles, and therefore a descendant of Gelon too?

We have only a few tidbits of information about the bulk of Archimedes' life, without any sense of order or chronology. We know nothing of his childhood; his mother is nameless. Of his education next to nothing, except that he travelled to Alexandria in Egypt at some point, which by that time was a leading centre of academic studies.

Then, as now, the extreme antiquity of Egyptian civilization elicited expectations of deep wisdom to go with it. But ancient Alexandria was far more a Greek city than an Egyptian one, having been founded at the end of the fourth century BCE by Alexander the Great to anchor his western dominions. The young Archimedes' priority would likely have been to network with the galaxy of leading minds that had gathered there at the invitation of the Ptolemaic kings. From the few pieces of correspondence we have, we know he made several lifelong contacts, including the mathematician Conon and astronomer Aristarchus, both of Samos; Conon's student and successor Dositheos of Pelusium; and Eratosthenes of Cyrene, the head librarian of the Great Library from 245 BCE to about 204 BCE.[5]

Whether the young Archimedes laid eyes on the Pyramids, or the wonders of Karnak and Thebes, can only be a matter of conjecture. Most likely he did travel upriver and witness at first hand how the Egyptians used regular inundations of the Nile to replenish their farmlands. The one invention often attributed to him in this period is the so-called 'Archimedes' screw': a water-lifting device composed of a spiral clad in a watertight wood or metal housing. One end of the device is placed in water, the other at an angle up to the level to be irrigated (forming the hypotenuse of a right-angled triangle). When the screw is turned – typically by foot – water is transported up successively higher 'chambers' formed by the rotating screw, until it is emptied at the higher level.

Both elegantly simple and devilishly effective, the screw pump may well not have been invented by Archimedes. The sources cited for this use Greek verbs that are ambiguous and could equally be read to mean he 'observed' or 'found' the pump in Egypt.[6] Indeed, it would be more surprising if the rich, ancient and technically capable hydraulic kingdoms of Mesopotamia and Egypt did *not* hit upon this method for lifting water far earlier. Most likely, versions of it were in use centuries before Archimedes saw it; screws cast in bronze may have been in use in Babylon as early as the time of King Sennacherib (705–681 BCE).[7] It is equally possible that the inspiration went in reverse: the geometry implicit in the device, its triangles and spirals, may have triggered a fascination with these shapes that ultimately influenced both Archimedes' practical innovations and his geometric research.

Of course it is still possible that Archimedes improved on or perfected the mechanism. In a larger sense, though, whether he originated the screw pump is less significant than the fact that it was so readily attributed to him in the first place. Crediting individual craftsmen (or women, for that matter) was by no means the norm throughout most of antiquity. Typically the patron who directed and paid the 'inventor' was given the credit, and that was usually a king or tyrant. What we begin to see with Archimedes, however, is the appearance in history of the archetypal engineer-innovator.[8] This continued with such figures as Ktesibius and Heron of Alexandria, and, after a long hiatus, giants like Leonardo, Brunelleschi, Edison and Tesla (many of whom explicitly hailed Archimedes as their inspiration). With the 'machinist' from Syracuse, we see the emergence of a different kind of actor in history: an individual who influenced events entirely by dint of technical genius.

After his time in Egypt Archimedes made his way back to Sicily. We do not know how old he was when he left Syracuse or when he returned. We do not know whether he stopped at any of the other scientific and cultural centres of the time, such as Athens, Pergamon or Rhodes. We do not even know such basic facts about his life as whether he was married or had children. A thin thread comprising statements by Cicero and Silius Italicus suggests he was 'humble and obscure', 'poor in this world's goods', but none of this specifies whether his relative poverty was by necessity, by choice or ginned up to contrast more dramatically with his brilliant mind.[9]

This is frustrating, but unfortunately par for the course when it comes to the major figures in Hellenistic science. We know similarly little about the personal lives of Eratosthenes (director of the Great Library and renowned measurer of the earth), Aristarchus (who first proposed a heliocentric cosmic system) or Theophrastus (successor to Aristotle at Athens's Lyceum and father of the science of botany). Compared to most of his contemporaries, Archimedes actually comes off somewhat favourably as regards preservation of certain anecdotes about his life, including the manner of his death.

We do know more about the history of his home city. And so, in the way of his approximation of the value of pi (π) in his treatise *Measurement of a Circle*, we can try to converge on a picture of him from both inside – that is, from known scraps of his biography – and from outside, the context of his life in Syracuse.[10]

Trinacria

Sicily is the largest island in the Mediterranean Sea and central to it, abutting both Italy and north Africa. Roughly defined by three capes in the southeast (Passero), northeast (Peloro) and west (Lilibeo), it was called 'Trinacria' by the Greeks. It is surely one of history's most on-the-nose ironies that its greatest geometer came from an island shaped like a triangle.

The Athenian general-historian Thucydides (fifth century BCE) and the Roman-era Greek geographer Strabo (*c.* 63 BCE–*c.* 24 CE) identify Sicily as the home of the Cyclops and the Laestrygonians of the *Odyssey*. In Homer's epic, the latter are a race of flesh-eating giants who hurl rocks at the hero's ship. When the first mainland Greeks arrived in Sicily in the eighth century BCE, they found the natives in the southeast corner of the island a bit more hospitable. Colonists from Corinth settled on an offshore island they called Ortygia ('Quail Island') in 733 BCE.[11] Ortygia was not only defensible, but situated between two natural harbours – an ideal refuge for mariners no matter which direction the wind was blowing. Etymologists differ over where the name 'Syracuse' came from, but a leading theory is that it derives from *Syraka*, the name of a swamp situated near the Great Harbour.

On seeing modern Siracusa for the first time, it is impossible to avoid the impression of a city blessed by geography. The island thrusts seaward like the prow of a ship, flaring enough in the centre to accommodate a lattice of avenues and cross-streets. In the southwest quarter rises the spring of Arethusa, a once-fresh (now somewhat brackish) source of water that helped the city stand strong against a series of epic sieges. In his *Metamorphoses*, Ovid tells the story of Arethusa, an Arcadian nymph who appealed to Artemis to help her escape the amorous attentions of the river-god Alpheus.[12] The goddess answers her pleas by transforming the perspiring nymph into a stream. She also keeps Alpheus from mingling his waters with hers, diverting Arethusa underground through 'caverns dark'. Arethusa emerges free and uncontaminated on Ortygia – a symbol not only of chastity preserved, but of pure Greekness flowing from the heart of the Peloponnese directly to Syracuse.

Today the Fountain of Arethusa is a fenced urban park, a limpid oasis hosting ducks and cats and one of the only stands of Egyptian papyrus in Europe.[13] No doubt it was something considerably more practical in Archimedes' time: in his youth he would have seen his neighbours drawing their drinking water from it, as well as diverting it for industrial uses. One might think he spared little thought for nymphs and amorous river-gods. The papyrus, however, might have inspired dreams of Egypt that were ultimately fulfilled when he reached Alexandria.

Sicily prior to Greek settlement must have seemed like a paradise compared to the Greek mainland. Where the latter was rocky, with relatively few major rivers or regions suitable for large-scale agriculture, Trinacria was amply blessed with both. Fine harbours on every coast offered access to seemingly inexhaustible fisheries. (Leaping dolphins on ancient Syracusan coins commemorated this abundance.) The island also offered the advantage of being lightly settled by native people, the Sicels, Sicans and Elymians – or at least according to the Greeks themselves. By the end of the seventh century BCE colonies had been established in the east (Naxos, by the Euboeans, Syracuse, by the Corinthians, Megara Hyblaea from Megara) and the south (Gela, by the Cretans). Those cities in turn spawned other settlements (Noto, Kamarina and Himera from Syracuse; Akragas from Gela; Selinus from Megara Hyblaea, among others).

Sicily at that time was like a controlled experiment where the question was posed: what could Greeks become if unshackled from the geographical limitations of old Greece? Within a few centuries the answer was *numerous* and *comfortable*, as the population and living standards on the island quickly exceeded those of the ancestral homelands. A stupefying abundance of food inspired the founding of the world's first school for professional chefs, in Syracuse in the fifth century BCE.[14] In what is perhaps the original manifestation of *la dolce vita*, Archestratus of Syracuse or Gela (*c.* 350 BCE) published the *Hedypatheia* (On the Sweet Life), a kind of poetic Baedeker surveying the gastronomical delights of the entire Greek world. Zest for life among the residents of Magna Graecia ('great Greece', as the Romans later called Sicily and neighbouring regions on the Italian mainland) was so pervasive that the philosopher Empedocles of Acragas declared, 'Sicilian Greeks built as if they would live forever and ate as if they would die tomorrow.'[15]

Alas, along with rich and independent, the Sicilian Greeks were, like Greeks everywhere, fractious. Sicily's patchwork of foundations, all owing cultural allegiance to different regions of the old country, guaranteed that the island was continually riven by conflict. These rivalries offered opportunities to outside powers to interfere in affairs on the island – most immediately to the Phoenicians, who established their own colonies in the west of the island, at Panormus (Palermo) and Soluntum, and to the Phoenician-descended maritime power of Carthage, which contended with Syracuse for dominance on the island for centuries. Ultimately, expansionist Rome exploited these rivalries so decisively that no independent Sicilian power ruled the island for another millennium. Thereafter Sicily was weakened to the point that it was conquered in turn by Germanic tribes, Byzantines, Muslims, Normans, the French and the Spanish, with most of these ruling the island for their own benefit, not for that of the people who lived there. Alas, the historical consequences of this sad trajectory are still with us today. Sicily and adjacent regions in the south of Italy are still among the poorest in the country when, judging from their historical fertility and resources, they should be among the richest.

The apogee of ancient Syracuse was arguably the zenith of Sicily herself. By the beginning of the fifth century BCE its population (including citizens, slaves and resident aliens) was already around 200,000 – a stupendous number for the time that made her comparable to Athens.[16] Conflict between the rich landowning classes and the masses led to civil unrest that opened up opportunities for political adventurers. One such man was Gelon, a cavalry commander who hailed originally from the island of Telos but earned distinction in the service of Syracuse's rival Gela, on the southern coast. When his sponsor Hippocrates fell in battle, Gelon deftly removed his heirs and assumed power over Gela himself.[17] He saw (and seized) an even bigger chance six years later, when elements of the Syracusan aristocracy were exiled by their subjects and appealed to Gela for help. Gelon was only too happy to use his army to restore the landowners of Trinacria's greatest city to their banquet couches. They in turn were only too grateful to recognize Gelon as *tyrant* (a word with oppressive connotations now but not necessarily in antiquity, equating more with 'usurper').

Indeed, Gelon became not only Syracuse's first tyrant, but the model of all who followed, including those who ruled during Archimedes' lifetime. Over the course of seven eventful years, he remade the city demographically and physically, exiling populist elements and resettling loyal citizens from Gela, building a wall around the city's first mainland quarter of Achradina ('place of the wild pears') and establishing the satellite settlements of Tyche and Neapolis on the high ground north of Ortygia. He also expanded Syracuse's navy, adding docks and berthing facilities at the small harbour. What was already one of the most powerful Greek cities became something of a military juggernaut; just a few years later, when the mainland Greeks faced imminent invasion by King Xerxes of Persia, they sent an embassy to Gelon, as his 'power was said to be very great, surpassing by far any power in Hellas [Greece]'.[18] In response, Gelon offered to lend a force of 200 triremes, 20,000 infantry, 2,000 horse, 2,000 archers and 2,000 slingers – in other words, a force of some 65,000 men in addition to whatever he would need to defend himself in Sicily.[19]

All those military assets turned out to be useful when Syracuse faced a foreign challenge of her own. In 480 BCE Carthaginians under Hamilcar launched a major invasion of Sicily. Though allegedly sent to restore an allied tyrant to the throne of Himera, on Sicily's north coast, Carthage's offensive was almost certainly timed to take advantage of the Greek world's preoccupation with repelling the Persians. They didn't count on Gelon. Rushing north, he routed Hamilcar's army, reportedly on the very same day the allied Greeks turned the tide on Xerxes at Salamis.

As the Athenians eventually did after Xerxes' defeat, Gelon used the financial windfall that followed his victory to bankroll a programme of civic building, including a new temple dedicated to Athena. Meanwhile, he humbly presented himself to the collected citizens of Syracuse, coming to the Assembly

> not only with no arms but not even wearing a tunic and clad only in a cloak, and stepping forward he rendered an account of his whole life and of all he had done for the Syracusans; and when the throng shouted its approval at each action he mentioned and showed especially its amazement that he had given himself unarmed into the hands of any who might wish to slay him, so far was he from being a victim of vengeance as a tyrant that they united in acclaiming him with one voice Benefactor and Saviour and King.[20]

Periods of tyranny alternated with phases more akin to democracy over the rest of the city's independent history. Ironically, it was during one of the liberal periods (the so-called 'Second Democracy', 466 BCE–405 BCE) that the original democracy, Athens, besieged Syracuse. The ensuing conflict became one of the darkest episodes in the histories of both cities. (So much for the truism that 'democracies never attack each other.') The details, though momentous, aren't strictly relevant here. What is germane is how that siege influenced how Syracuse planned to meet any future attacks. The Athenians were repelled in 413 BCE only after a long, attritional struggle, and only after the defenders received outside help. Indeed, they came within an ace of trapping the entire city behind a series of counter-walls, the completion of which was prevented by a feverish programme of counter-counter-wall-building by the Syracusans.[21]

It comes as little surprise, then, that after Syracuse's next major tyrant, Dionysius i, toppled the democracy, he went on to build many, many fortifications on the high ground of Epipolae. The full Dionysian circuit was not only vast, covering 27 kilometres (17 mi.), but completed in just six years. He also built the first version of the Euryalos Castle, a nearly impregnable fortress set on the highest point of the plateau. No power was ever going to box Syracuse in with siege walls again. When the Romans came two centuries later, they didn't try.

Another Dionysian innovation was the development of powerful siege engines. While there are earlier references to machines devised to propel stones, Dionysius apparently launched one of history's first known military research programmes.[22] Specialists were organized into 'teams' that were assigned discrete goals which, when pieced together, resulted in novel weapons. These included naval vessels that were propelled by more than the one man per oar that was standard in classical triremes, yielding a more powerful punch when they rammed their enemies.

Dionysius' boffins devised the first Greek catapults – basically, scaled-up versions of the crossbows carried by individual soldiers. The arms races that followed between the successors of Alexander the Great ultimately led to more powerful forms of artillery that were based not on the bending of flexible bows but on torsion, the force stored in a flexible material like rope when it is twisted. By the end of the Hellenistic period in the first century BCE, catapults were in use that were capable of propelling 20-kilogram (44 lb) stones hundreds of metres.

As the range and power of these machines steadily increased, the advantage began to swing away from the defenders of cities and towards the besiegers. Aristotle sounded the alarm as early as the mid-fourth century BCE, when he argued that advances in siegecraft had made traditional notions of military virtue obsolete:

> The superiority of the besiegers may be and often is too much both for ordinary human valor . . . if they are to be saved and to escape defeat and outrage, the strongest wall will be the truest soldierly precaution, more especially now that missiles and siege engines have been brought to such perfection.[23]

Aristotle might as well have been talking directly to Dionysius, and to Archimedes later on, when he advised, 'For as the assailants of a city do all they can to gain an advantage, so the defenders should make use of any means of defense which have been already discovered, *and should devise and invent others*, for when men are well prepared, no enemy even thinks of attacking them' (emphasis added).

Though they weren't the sole reason, advances in *poliorcetics* ('city-busting') contributed to the historical decline of the individual Greek city-states like Athens and Corinth, which could no longer compete against the resources of kingdom-sized powers like Macedon, Carthage, the Seleucid Empire or Roman Italy. (Demetrius I, a king of Macedon, literally bore the sobriquet Πολιορκητής – the 'besieger'.)

The survival of these smaller polities increasingly depended on careful management of their relations with their neighbours, a diplomatic knack perfectly embodied by Syracuse's last great tyrant, and Archimedes' patron, Hieron II.

The Giants

'In all the earth round which the Sun drives his chariot,' wrote the Roman epic poet and politician Silius Italicus in his *Punica*, 'no city at that time could rival Syracuse.'[24] The city continued to grow and prosper through the fourth century BCE, as rich and populous as the rising Roman power to her north. Alas, despite the city's technological prowess, she never really developed the tools – the institutions and traditions – that she needed in order to rule herself peacefully.

It wasn't all wine and architecture for the ageing Dionysius. With time, he became so terrified of assassination that he refused to trust his barber with scissors. He neglected the education of his son because 'fearing that, if he should get wisdom and associate with men of sense, he would plot against him and rob him of his power, [so he] used to keep [his son] closely shut up at home.' Instead of honing the skills of statecraft, the younger Dionysius spent his formative years whittling little wooden models of carts and furniture. His tastes soon turned to even less constructive pursuits: while the father was off erecting fortifications, the son achieved the dubious distinction of keeping a single drinking party going for ninety days in a row.[25]

Dionysius II succeeded his father in 367 BCE. By that time wiser heads prevailed on the young tyrant to invite a certain special guest to instruct him on the principles of good governance. This guest turned out to be Plato himself. The philosopher was received at first with great honours, and soon became something of an obsession of his young student. The tutorship soured, however, as Plato tried to discipline Dionysius' mind with geometry. 'God', the philosopher is said to have declared, 'is always doing geometry.' But Dionysius II was content to leave geometry to God. The political climate soon became actively dangerous and the philosopher was obliged to flee. Plato later came to regret his efforts to bring some kind of enlightened rule to the Syracusans:

> For [no man] will, with his eyes open, make his way by [sound] steps like these to a power which will be fraught with destruction to himself and his descendants for all time; but he will advance towards constitutional government and the framing of the justest and best laws, reaching these ends without executions and murders even on the smallest scale.[26]

Neither Syracuse nor Sicily was destined for leadership 'without murders'. More autocrats followed through the rest of the fourth century BCE. Yet another democratic experiment flourished under Timoleon, an immigrant from the old country of Corinth, but fell in short order. It was followed by another tyrant, Agathocles, and another after that, Hicetas. It was probably under the latter that the child Archimedes was born to Phidias the astronomer – a child who was destined for greatness, but never lived a minute of his life under any kind of rule but autocracy.

The history of the city in the third century BCE unfolded largely under the shadow of Roman expansion. Alarmed by the rise of the upstart to the north, the Greek cities of Italy invited one of the most gifted military Greek commanders of his time, Pyrrhus of Epirus, to intervene. Pyrrhus defeated the Romans at the Battle of Asculum, northeast of Rome, but at such a heavy price that it became the archetype of self-defeating (Pyrrhic) victory. Seeking easier pickings in Sicily – 'Sicily is near, and holds out her hands to us, an island abounding in wealth and men, and very easy to capture' – Pyrrhus accepted a Syracusan invitation to drive the Carthaginians out of western Sicily.[27] Again he found initial success, beating the Carthaginians back to their stronghold on the west coast of the island. But he could not consolidate his political position in Syracuse and soon was on his way back to mainland Italy.

More consequential than any of his victories, Pyrrhus left behind one of his supporting generals, a native Syracusan named Hieron. As noted above, he was illegitimate, but also claimed descent along Gelon's illustrious ancestral line, the Deinomenids. This odd combination of illegitimacy and dynasty apparently gave Hieron a talent both for command and for breaking rules. He exploited both qualities to good effect in campaigns against the Mamertines, a mercenary faction that had taken up residence in Messana (now Messina), at Sicily's northeast tip. After driving Mamertine raiders out of Syracusan territory, the city offered Hieron the post of supreme commander, a position from which a royal throne was but a short step. By 270 BCE he ruled Syracuse as Hieron II. On his kinsman's ascension to the throne, Archimedes would have been seventeen years old.

Hieron backed the Carthaginians at first, but soon made peace with Rome. On an island of perpetually shifting alliances, Hieron's Syracuse became one of Rome's most steadfast partners, supplying ships and docking facilities and otherwise sticking by the latter's side for more than fifty years. Rome, for her part, left Syracuse in control of southeast Sicily. This time under Rome's wing afforded Hieron the luxury to develop Syracuse's economy, patronize the arts and, in the person of Archimedes, sponsor advances in science and technology.

The splendour of Syracuse during this period can perhaps best be appreciated by Cicero's description of the riches Verres stripped from her.[28] The city was beautified with architecture, paintings and sculpture of the first quality, including fine portraits of the poet Sappho and the gods Paeon, Libera and Aristaeus; a massive series of paintings in the Temple of Athena, portraying a cavalry battle waged by the tyrant Agathocles (reminiscent, one supposes, of the famous Alexander Mosaic from Pompeii); a set of exquisite temple doors made of ivory and incised gold; a series of 27 portraits of great Syracusans ('which delighted one, not only by the skill of the painter, but also by reminding us of the men, and by enabling us to recognize their persons,' raves Cicero). Verres not only made off with these riches, the orator charges, but used some of them to decorate the house of a prostitute in Rome.

Somewhat more muscular evidence of Hieron's legacy was too massive for even Verres to haul away. In the suburb of Neapolis, not far from the theatre (which Hieron also renovated, expanding and perfecting its acoustics), one can still find the foundations of the Altar of Hieron II. This elongated structure, almost 200 metres (650 ft) long, is what remains of the largest sacrificial altar known from antiquity. Dedicated to Zeus, it was large enough to accommodate the sacrifice of no fewer than 450 bulls. How much piety does this amount to? By rough estimate, if one steer yields some 200 kilograms (440 lb) of beef, a full-blown sacrifice at Hieron's altar would produce some 90 metric tons, or enough to serve a decent-sized steak to almost half a million people.[29] Some estimates of Syracuse's total population in this period, incidentally, run to 500,000.

These numbers, stupendous as they are, do not even begin to address the artistic wonder the altar must have presented, with a course of carved triglyphs running the entire length, and carved telamones (giants) supporting staircases to the higher levels (all lost now). By comparison, the remains of Rome's Ara Pacis and Pergamon's Great Altar are mere garden follies.

Hieron's pact with Rome gave the king the breathing space to build up Syracuse's economic base. The natural advantages of her double harbour and the fertility of her soils combined to make the city a major food exporter. As noted by Cicero, a tax of 10 per cent was levied on this massive trade, providing all the cash he needed to make Syracuse the envy of the Greek world.

Hieron also grasped the value of economic soft power. In addition to offering wheat to Greek cities suffering famine, he sent 125,000 bushels of grain to Rome after her defeat by Hannibal at Lake Trasimene.[30] Yet he also aided the Carthaginians in an earlier crisis, rationalizing that Carthage's mercantile power ultimately benefited his import trade.[31] As noted by Polybius, though he was allied with Rome, Hieron understood the importance of keeping Carthage around as a counterweight to his aggressive senior partner.

He followed the fashion of other Hellenistic rulers, such as the Ptolemies of Egypt, in patronizing artists, poets and writers whose presence would burnish their cities' renown. These included Timaeus of Tauromenium, regarded as one of the most influential Hellenistic historians, and Syracuse's own Theocritus, father of ancient pastoral poetry. The poet repaid his patron by gushing, 'the fame of Hiero(n) may minstrels bear aloft, across the Scythian sea, and where Semiramis reigned, that built the mighty wall, and made it fast with slime for mortar.'[32] But by far the most consequential of Hieron's clients was Archimedes.

The Lever of Heaven

As we have noted, Archimedes may have been a kinsman – possibly the nephew – of the tyrant/king. What this meant in practical terms is mostly a matter of conjecture. It might have afforded Archimedes certain privileges, such as easy access to the palace, but it doesn't necessarily mean they were boon companions or even on particularly friendly terms. There is a historical tradition that Archimedes served the crown in some official way, such as sitting on a 'council of friends and relatives', but there is no record of this in the primary sources.[33] The mathematician dedicates the *Sand-Reckoner* to Hieron's son Gelon, in a tone that suggests that Hieron had raised an heir well able to follow geometrical reasoning (contrast this to Plato's exasperation with the young Dionysius II). We also know that Hieron turned to Archimedes for a solution to his suspicions about a certain gold crown (see below); on the assumption that not all instances of consultation were recorded, it is likely that this is not the only occasion where he sought Archimedes' help.

One other episode is well attested: at some point, probably in the middle third of Hieron's reign, Archimedes conducted a demonstration of the power of leverage that altered the pair's relationship. Plutarch writes:

> Archimedes, who was a kinsman and friend of King Hiero, wrote to him that with any given force it was possible to move any given weight; and emboldened, as we are told, by the strength of his demonstration, he declared that, if there were another world, and he could go to it, he could move this. Hiero was astonished, and begged him to put his proposition into execution, and show him some great weight moved by a slight force. Archimedes therefore fixed upon a three-masted merchantman of the royal fleet, which had been dragged ashore by the great labours of many men, and after putting on board many passengers and the customary freight, he seated himself at a distance from her, and without any great effort, but quietly setting in motion with his hand a system of compound pulleys, drew her towards him smoothly and evenly, as though she were gliding through the water.[34]

If we take Plutarch literally, it appears that Archimedes and Hieron were at least in written contact, and that the former was not above a certain conspicuous confidence, if not boastfulness. This is not surprising given what we have of Archimedes' other correspondence, such as a letter to Eratosthenes that adopts a tone of barely implicit superiority: 'Seeing moreover in you, as I say, an earnest student . . . I thought fit to write out for you and explain in detail in the same book the peculiarity of a certain method, by which it will be possible for you to get a start.'[35] In Archimedes we are in the presence of someone very comfortably aware of his own genius.

Hieron was, in any case, impressed. Says Plutarch,

> Amazed at [the levering of the ship], then, and comprehending the power of his art, the king persuaded Archimedes to prepare for him offensive and defensive engines to be used in every kind of siege warfare. These he had never used himself, because he spent the greater part of his life in freedom from war and amid the festal rites of peace; but at the present time his apparatus stood the Syracusans in good stead, and, with the apparatus, its fabricator.

As the Neoplatonist philosopher Proclus (412–485 CE) has it, the king declared, after witnessing the launching, that 'From this day forth we must believe everything that Archimedes says.'[36]

That Hieron asked Archimedes to apply his ingenuity to engines of war (offensive and defensive), and that Archimedes complied, are usually reported by modern historians as if they deserve no further comment. But they should prompt certain questions. First, against whom did Hieron believe Syracuse needed to prepare a defence? Carthage is the obvious answer, though one wonders why Hieron didn't believe his pact with Rome was sufficient guarantee of his security. That the king wanted an insurance policy in case the alliance broke down must be a possibility. Tyrants don't get to be tyrants without a certain degree of prudent mistrust, after all.

But why did Archimedes take up the challenge? Given the entrenched image of a man so preoccupied with his abstract studies that he barely functioned as an adult (neglecting his hygiene, for example), that he would suddenly throw himself into the design and building of war machines sounds like a radical departure. Notwithstanding the cliché of the lone genius tossing off practical designs in his idle moments between abstract proofs, developing his military technology (indeed, developing any military technology) requires field supervision, evaluation, adjustment and re-evaluation. There is no value to a weapon, after all, if it doesn't work when it is most needed. At risk of putting too sharp a point on it, that Archimedes designed a defence of Syracuse without being closely invested in its deployment is a fantasy.

Did he make this effort just because Hieron, his sovereign and relative, asked him to? Possibly. It is not beyond plausibility that Archimedes understood that he was very lucky in his choice

3 Archimedes supervising the construction of Syracuse's defences, in Giovanni Pastrone's silent film epic *Cabiria* (1914).

of lifetime. His luxury to think and work in peace was directly related to the stability of Hieron's exceptionally long reign, and Archimedes almost certainly knew it. He wouldn't have had to look much beyond Sicily to see how chronic civil unrest and warfare would affect his freedom to work.

And indeed, the thoroughness of Archimedes' defensive works suggests that they were designed in much better than obliging, perfunctory fashion. The task seems to have been done in much the same spirit as his exhibition of moving the ship – spectacularly, and 'with the left and only hand', no less.[37] It is tempting to imagine that launching the ship was, at least in part, a demonstration of the services Archimedes did not just consent to provide, but wanted to. Plutarch's absent-minded professor may actually conceal a much more worldly, politically savvy Archimedes, who understood that the right levers in the right hands could move not only the heaviest of objects, but the minds of kings.[38]

Fishers of Men

On the final chapter in Archimedes' life we have just a handful of classical sources. In addition to Plutarch (c. 45–125 CE), we have accounts of the Roman siege of Syracuse by Polybius (c. 203 BCE–120 BCE) and Livy (59 BCE–17 CE). Polybius is chronologically closest to the actual events and among modern scholars the most respected historian of the three, but important parts of the story, including Archimedes' death, are missing. Livy's account of the campaign is the most detailed. Plutarch is the better storyteller and more concerned with relating the characters behind the events. Broadly, however, the main sources are in close agreement on the facts.

Plutarch (Lucius Mestrius Plutarchus) is such an important source for Archimedes that it is easy to forget he is not the subject of Plutarch's account. The intended hero is Marcus Claudius

Marcellus, the Roman general who led the assault that resulted in Archimedes' death.[39] So while Archimedes' historical legacy is now magnitudes greater than Marcellus', he appears here only as a supporting character in Marcellus' story.

In 214 BCE, as Hannibal menaced Italy, a pro-Carthaginian faction in Syracuse saw a chance to unravel the city's alliance with Rome. Marcellus, after some successes against the rearguard of Hannibal's army, was selected to command the Roman force sent to return Syracuse to the fold. A two-pronged attack by land and sea was launched, with Marcellus personally leading the amphibious attack on the sea walls and his colleague Appius Claudius the land assault on the city's northern gates. The Roman army was battle-hardened after years of war with the Carthaginians, and outnumbered the defenders. Many of Marcellus' men, moreover, were disgraced survivors of the catastrophic Roman defeat at Cannae in 216 BCE, and had much to prove.

None of them expected to run into the buzz-saw of resistance engineered by Archimedes. As the Romans approached, the mathematician unleashed a plethora of ingenious weapons that made the small Syracusan army seem much bigger than it was. Volleys of missiles from artillery, cleverly calibrated to hit targets at any range, mowed the Romans down no matter how far they stood from the walls. Legionaries who survived to reach the fortifications were greeted by another horror: a system of apertures big enough to shoot through but too small for the Romans to climb though. Through these embrasures the Syracusans were safe to work their 'scorpions', a kind of anti-personnel catapult that launched salvos of arrows. They also practised 'catch and release' on the Romans using a grappling hook fastened to the end of a beam that was projected over the wall. When the defenders managed to latch on to a Roman, they used the principle of the lever to fish him, armour and all, high into the air – then drop him.[40]

The attack on the sea walls of Achradina fared no better. In addition to overwhelming numbers, the Roman fleet brought to the fight a leverage-based superweapon of its own. Marcellus' 'rolling elevatable scaling ladder' was itself based on Archimedean principles, and so massive it had to be mounted on two ships lashed together, catamaran-style.[41] When this *sambuca* (so named because it resembled a long-necked musical instrument of the same name) reached the walls, its crews erected the ladder using a system of pulleys. Troops were then sent up and over the battlements.

That was the theory. When the *sambuca* and the other Roman ships approached the seaward walls of Syracuse, however, they were scattered by long-range artillery that threw heavy stones and probably incendiary missiles. Vessels that survived to reach the walls were attacked by the ancestors of anti-ship mines – iron hooks ('tricuspidae') that were pre-planted on the sea bottom and winched up under the Roman keels, upending and sinking them.[42]

Others were hooked by larger versions of the anti-personnel grappling devices used against Appius' troops. Projected over the walls, these massive levering machines supposedly used counterweights to lift whole ships out of the water, suspending them by their prows. The creaking wooden masses full of screaming, terrified men were then cut loose and capsized. Though controversy seems to adhere especially to tales of Archimedes' alleged use of burning mirrors, accounts of an 'iron hand' or 'claw' of Archimedes, capable of snatching whole ships of 100 tonnes from the sea, seems as much the stuff of pure fantasy. And yet most historians are inclined to believe them – perhaps because they are so perfectly consistent with Archimedes' boast that, with a lever long enough and a place to stand, he could move anything.

Reconciling all this with the existing topography of Syracuse is not straightforward. As the action is described by the historians, we need to envision the Roman ships sailing virtually within touching distance of the city's seaward walls. In most places this seems physically unlikely, given that the sea floor either slopes very gradually downward from the base of the walls, leaving almost no draught for fully laden warships, or is littered with boulders that would have ripped the keels out of any large vessels attempting to sail close. Even allowing for the possibility that the waterline has changed since Archimedes' time, the Roman fleet could have attacked only along a few select stretches of wall. This at least may have helped in the planning for Archimedes' defence, because he would have known the exact places with water deep enough for ships to approach, and placed his machines accordingly.

And indeed, Polybius and Livy report that the Roman fleet mounted their attack along the seaward defences at Achradina, 'where the wall reaches down to the very edge of the sea'.[43] This detail narrows down the location of the action to somewhat less than a kilometre of coastline between the Stoa Scytice and the small harbour north of Ortygia. Assuming that Archimedes positioned his devices to cover every possible approach to that exposed stretch of wall, it has been estimated that the defence would have required 25 machines.[44]

Though widely accepted, there is reason to suspect the primary accounts of the claw of Archimedes are somewhat sensationalized. For starters, the mechanical stresses of lifting ships out of the water would have have been so enormous as to demand wooden structures made of the biggest trees on earth, such as 'Australian mountain-ash eucalypts, North American sequoias, or North American Douglas firs' – obviously, species unavailable to the Syracusans.[45] Even if they managed to cobble together adequate equipment by bundling trunks of lighter timber, the kind of massive wooden structures necessary for the job would have been easy for the enemy to spot, making any kind of tactical surprise extremely unlikely.

The conventional stories look even more dubious, moreover, when we realize that it was not even necessary to lift the Roman ships clear of the water to destroy them. As accounts of whole fleets lost in storms during the Punic Wars attest, Roman vessels of the time could hardly have been called seaworthy under the fairest of circumstances. Their long, canoe-like profiles, extensive and top-heavy superstructures, and the multitude of holes for the oars made them vulnerable to overturning or swamping even in moderately heavy seas. The inherent instability of the quinquereme was no doubt something of which Archimedes was keenly aware – he wrote two entire treatises, *On Floating Bodies I* and *II*, that exhaustively explored the stability of paraboloid sections in fluids. He would undoubtedly have known that a force applied laterally to a full-laden warship, of the right magnitude and in the right place, could tip it over. Among the few modern attempts to model the functioning of Archimedes' claw, one concluded that it would have been far easier to wreck a ship by simply snagging it from the side and lifting just a bit: 'It was not necessary to raise the ship from the water at all, it simply tipped over like an unbalanced canoe.'[46] Indeed, just catching and arresting a moving ship might have been enough to flip it, as it might have been unbalanced by the lateral force of the anchored 'iron hand', combined with its own momentum. No sequoias or Herculean hoists necessary.

Whether they literally plucked Roman ships into the air or just gave them a well-placed nudge, the psychological impact of the Syracusan defences was every bit as devastating as the physical damage. So ubiquitous did Archimedes' mind seem, so cleverly disposed to anticipate any countermeasure, that the Romans became terrified at every bit of rope or stick of timber projecting a little over the wall: '"There it is," they cried, "Archimedes is training some engine upon us!" and turned their backs and fled.'[47]

Marcellus, a seasoned commander who had killed a Gallic king in single combat and helped to keep the undefeated Hannibal off-balance in Italy, decided that he had never fought anything like the mind of Archimedes. Plutarch has him despair (somewhat implausibly), 'Let us stop fighting against this geometrical Briareus, who uses our ships like cups to ladle water from the sea ... and with the many missiles which he shoots against us all at once, outdoes the hundred-handed monsters of mythology.' Polybius' version is more becoming of a terse Roman commander: 'Archimedes uses my ships to ladle seawater into his wine cups, but my sambuca band is flogged out of the banquet in disgrace.'[48]

The analogy with Briareus, the mythical creature with one hundred arms and fifty heads, is an apt one, as Plutarch and Polybius both report that the entire Syracusan resistance seemed to operate seamlessly, under the direction of one mind ('Archimedes' literally means 'master planner' or 'master counsellor'). Indeed, only Archimedes' mechanisms seemed to figure in the struggle; conventional weapons like bows and javelins, wielded by mere mortals, were not even considered worth mentioning.[49] The Romans anticipated a quick campaign that would last perhaps a week.[50] Instead, they were forced to set up a siege that lasted more than two years.

The effectiveness of Archimedes' defence of Syracuse is usually attributed to his ingenious devices. But it was innovative in terms of tactics as well. In modern military doctrine, the term 'echelonment of fires' means 'the execution of a schedule of fires fired from the highest caliber to the lowest caliber weapon, based on risk-estimate distances and weapons-system range capabilities, as the maneuver force moves toward an objective.'[51] In other words, by using different classes of ranged weapons to attack the enemy at every anticipated distance, Archimedes kept the approaching Romans under an assault so constant it sapped their numbers and their willingness to fight. Archimedes' echeloning of fires from catapults and scorpions was a tactic that any modern artillery officer would recognize and emulate. He was just centuries ahead of them all.

Meanwhile, the 'master planner' at the centre of all this destruction was said to be a quiet, modest figure, serenely detached from the consequences of his own ingenuity:

Archimedes possessed such a lofty spirit, so profound a soul, and such a wealth of scientific theory, that although his inventions had won for him a name and fame for super-human sagacity, he would not consent to leave behind him any treatise on this subject, but regarding the work of an engineer and every art that ministers to the needs of life as ignoble and vulgar, he devoted his earnest efforts only to those studies the subtlety and charm of which are not affected by the claims of necessity.[52]

There is reason to believe Plutarch exaggerates this detachment; it is not true, for instance, that he left behind no treatises on practical things. But there is a certain plausibility in Archimedes stepping back from the immediate task of defending the city. First, because he was in his seventies. Second, because, like one of his geometric proofs, the real work went into the preparation, the marshalling of axioms and principles that have their own, incontestable power. After he had set up Syracuse's defences (the *proposition*), demonstrating their efficacy (the *proof*) to the Romans was something of an afterthought, a mere matter of educating them.

The Romans eventually prevailed only because a stretch of wall was left under-defended during a festival of Artemis. This small opening was all Marcellus' troops needed to take the upper city (Achradina, Neapolis and so on). From there, Marcellus allegedly looked down on Ortygia and wept for its impending fate. The island held out for a while, but fell when a foreign mercenary accepted a bribe to open the gate near the Fountain of Arethusa. Notwithstanding his tears, and despite his orders that no Syracusan citizen should be attacked, Marcellus couldn't keep his legions from their customary reward. According to Livy, the sack of Syracuse yielded as much booty as the fall of Carthage, a maritime and commercial superpower, was to yield at her destruction by Rome in 146 BCE.[53]

In the Head, Not the Lines

Sometime between the invasion of the upper city and the final sack – the sources are not clear exactly when or where – Archimedes met his end. Marcellus had apparently issued a standing order that the mathematician be captured alive. But as Livy reports, 'Archimedes, in all the uproar which the alarm of a captured city could produce in the midst of plundering soldiers dashing about, was intent upon the figures which he had traced in the dust and was slain by a soldier, not knowing who he was.'[54] This certainly sounds in keeping with the distracted genius described by Plutarch, who would trace geometric figures in the oil with which his body was anointed.

The latter reports two other versions of the story: in the second, the soldier recognized Archimedes, and the old man did indeed acknowledge the soldier's demand. But when he begged only for a little time to finish the demonstration he was sketching, the impatient soldier drew his sword and killed him. In the third version Archimedes agreed to go to Marcellus, but on the way,

> Archimedes was carrying to Marcellus some of his mathematical instruments, such as sun-dials and spheres and quadrants, by means of which he made the magnitude of the Sun appreciable to the eye, some soldiers fell in with him, and thinking that he was carrying gold in the box, slew him.[55]

Which story is the most likely? Livy's depends on believing that the Roman soldier did not recognize Archimedes at all, even though Marcellus ordered the capture of a certain elderly Greek geometer, and the victim was discovered *actively doing geometry* at that very moment. In story number two, the soldier recognizes Archimedes but simply liquidates a valuable prisoner – indeed one who amounted to a strategic asset for Rome – simply because he was lackadaisical in responding to orders. This doesn't pass the smell test. Number three, by portraying Archimedes led through chaotic streets with an expensive-looking box, motivates his murder a bit more plausibly. But it ultimately still suffers from a similar objection: certainly, if it was generally understood that Marcellus wanted the old man captured alive, any properly self-interested soldier would know that the reward for capturing Archimedes would exceed the value of a few shiny gizmos.

It is at least conceivable that Archimedes simply kept the soldier cooling his heels too long. In the general uproar of Syracuse's sack, the Roman might have been concerned that someone else would come in, possibly of higher rank, and steal his reward. Where Plutarch puts the encounter in somewhat genteel terms, with Archimedes 'beseeching' the soldier for a little more time, more likely angry words were exchanged. The most popular tradition has Archimedes begging 'Don't disturb my circles.'[56] Tzetzes reports the somewhat more testy 'Man, keep away from my diagram!';[57] he also has Archimedes crying out, 'Someone, bring me one of my machines!', possibly a weapon to use against the intruder. Cassius Dio (c. 155–c. 235 CE) reportedly has him daring his assailant, 'Hit me in my head, not in my lines!'[58] Insofar as something Archimedes said may have triggered his Roman visitor, this may be a rare instance where the Byzantine sources are closer to the spirit of ancient events than the classical ones. And if Archimedes really did cry out for a weapon to defend himself, this is clearly a far more militant, cantankerous Archimedes than the serene, divinely removed genius of Plutarch.[59]

The apparently haphazard circumstances around the death of Archimedes have had the effect of inspiring other, more outré theories about what 'really' happened. An Italian historian published a paper in 2010 asserting that Archimedes was a victim of 'state-sponsored murder', which the Romans and their apologists conspired to cover up with crocodile tears about the despair of

Marcellus and a fine funeral.[60] If you tour the very informative Archimedes Technopark outside Siracusa today, you will hear tell of how the Syracusans themselves killed Archimedes in order to prevent his secrets from falling into enemy hands. Though interesting, these theories share the fact that neither is supported by anything but the threadbare nature of the primary sources. What 'state-sponsored murder' of an obvious military asset like Archimedes means in the context of war is debatable. And it is hard not to wonder why, if the Syracusans killed Archimedes, Romans and the pro-Roman historians would oblige in shifting blame on themselves.

Whichever version (if, indeed, any) resembles the truth, the episode has resonated through the centuries as an archetypal instance of stupidity assassinating wisdom. (Other candidates include the burning of the Great Library of Alexandria and the murder of Hypatia by a Christian mob.) The death of Archimedes became a piquant symbol of the impermanence of even the most profound human achievements. Edouard Vimont's late nineteenth-century image is typical: Archimedes crumpled on the floor while the soldier, the very personification of brute ignorance, in lion skin and what appears to be a lizard's tail, shoves an armillary sphere aside to get at his victim.

More informative is a mosaic, said to have been recovered from the buried Roman city of Herculaneum, that shows the key moment of the soldier demanding and Archimedes refusing (illus. 5). Though the mosaic itself may date only from the Renaissance, Eduard Jan Dijksterhuis notes an important detail that suggests an older inspiration: Archimedes is not scratching diagrams on a dirt floor, which is inherently unlikely for the complex figures typical of his work, but using a tabletop tray filled with fine sand or dust called an *abacus* (like the calculating instrument).[61] That the mathematician would snarl at an armed Roman soldier over mere lines scratched in a dirt floor makes sense only if we wish to emphasize

4 'Death of Archimedes', engraving after Edouard Vimont, from John Lord, *Beacon Lights of History*, vol. III (1888).

the fleeting nature of human endeavour (for example, Jesus, 'every one that heareth these sayings of mine, and doeth them not, shall be likened unto a foolish man, which built his house upon the sand' (Matthew 7:26)). The historical Archimedes almost certainly had better equipment to support his work, and was probably not shy about keeping it out of ignorant hands.

The sources also agree on the immediate consequences of Archimedes' death. Marcellus was much distressed, and not just because a valuable captive had been lost. The general 'was afflicted at his death ... and sought out the kindred of Archimedes and paid them honour'.[62] While we have no information about Archimedes' family, the fact that both Plutarch and Tzetzes specifically mention relatives suggests some did survive in the city. Marcellus' attempts at making redress to his kin is in keeping with ancient conceptions of justice: compensating the family for their loss was as important, if not more so, as directly punishing the killer. (On the matter of punishment, Plutarch says only that Marcellus 'turned away' from Archimedes' murderer 'as from a polluted person'.)[63]

Marcellus not only sought out the family and honoured them, but provided that the body be deposited with dignity in the tomb of his fathers. Tzetzes, quoting an earlier source, describes Archimedes being laid to rest 'in the company of the best of the citizens and all of the Romans'.[64] This is the kind of scene we would like to think furnished a fitting endpoint to the years' long siege: conquerors and conquered gathered together amid the monuments of illustrious Syracusans, observing the burial rites of the one man all of them could agree to honour.

One detail would have made Archimedes' grave unique: 'He is said to have asked his kinsmen and friends to place over the grave where he should be buried a cylinder enclosing a sphere, with

5 Mosaic depicting the death of Archimedes, 18th century, possibly inspired by a Hellenistic original.

an inscription giving the proportion by which the containing solid exceeds the contained.'[65] This would have been a reference to Archimedes' proof, described in his first treatise, *On the Sphere and the Cylinder*, that a sphere enclosed by a cylinder with a base and height exactly the same as the diameter of the circle has exactly two-thirds the volume and surface area of the cylinder. Considering the complexity of Archimedes' other achievements, both as abstract mathematician and as practical innovator, that he chose this rather simple geometrical relation as his eternal monument sounds curious to modern ears. But as we explore the more metaphysical bases underlying Archimedes' work, we will see that this ratio of basic shapes, in its simplicity and its purity, was actually an inspired choice to represent his legacy.

How the tomb actually looked can only be guessed at based on impressions from the few sources that mention it. There are two practical possibilities given the craft and practices of the time: either the sphere and cylinder were represented in two dimensions (as in a carving), or in three (as a sculpture in-the-round or raised relief). The former begs the question of how the three-dimensionality of

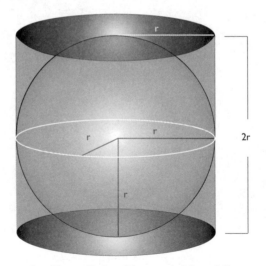

6 Sphere enclosed by a cylinder of the same height and diameter.

the figures would have been represented, in addition to the simple problem of how Cicero could have found it if the carving was over-grown by vegetation. Cicero's description – 'I observed a small column standing out a little above the briars, with the figure of a sphere and a cylinder upon it' – seems to suggest, if only vaguely, a sculpture.[66]

How it represented a sphere nestled inside a solid cylinder is another open and probably unanswerable question. (After all, if the sphere was completely hidden inside the cylinder, the reference to the ratio would have been lost.) One possibility suggested by Derek J. de Solla Price – that half the cylinder was cut away to reveal the sphere inside[67] – is interesting, insofar as it solves the representation problem, and raises the intriguing possibility that Archimedes' final visual testament inspired greater, larger and more enduring works to come.

Leveraging the Lever

As Archimedes left nothing behind to account for his wartime engineering, we can only speculate on what inspired his defence of Syracuse. This, at least, does not demand much imagination: many of the spectacular devices he unleashed on the Romans – the claw, the scorpion, the tricuspidae – operated on the principle of one of the most ancient mechanisms known to humankind.

In his time in Egypt Archimedes could not have helped notice how important the lever was in moving and raising heavy objects. The natives used levers to lift and adjust the positions of large blocks of stone for construction of pyramids and temples. Even more ubiquitous was the shaduf, a device for lifting water that consisted of a pole mounted horizontally on a pivot, with a bucket on one end and a counterweight at the other. After lowering the bucket into the water to fill it, the user takes advantage of the counterweight to help lift the full bucket. The origin of shadufs is lost in the mists of prehistory, but they have been a common sight in Egypt, Mesopotamia and India ever since. Archimedes almost certainly encountered them at first hand on his trip to Alexandria.

How levers work has never been a mystery. In its most abstract form, a lever can be represented by a line that pivots on a point (the fulcrum) somewhere along its length. Applying a downward force on one end of the lever causes the opposite to rise. A load on one end of the beam, such as a block of stone, or a bucket of water in a shaduf, can therefore be lifted by pressing down on the opposite end. Two loads of equal weight can be balanced if the fulcrum is placed at a point exactly between them. So much is obvious to anyone who has played on a see-saw in a playground.

Things began to get interesting – and useful – when people realized that a heavy load can be moved (or balanced) by a lighter one, provided the heavy one is placed closer to the fulcrum. Modern mathematicians would express this relationship in terms of an equation, but the ancient Greeks rarely did this. Instead, they would think of it in terms of a proportion:

$$H/h : l/L$$

Here, H is the heavy load, h the lighter load, L the distance from the fulcrum to H, and l the distance to h. A lever balances exactly when the ratio of the heavier load to the lighter is proportional to the lighter's distance to the heavier. For example, an 18-kilogram (40 lb) load will be balanced by a 9-kilogram (20 lb) one if the latter is twice as far from the fulcrum:

$$18 \ kg/9 \ kg : 60 \ cm/30 \ cm$$

The units, of course, do not matter in this proportion – at least in principle. With a long enough lever and a stable fulcrum, the relationship works just as well at the scale of metres, miles or light years. Any weight, no matter how stupendous, can theoretically be lifted. The Egyptians used levers to lift and position stone blocks weighing tens of tons – though that does not exhaust the potential of this simple device. A very clever mouse could theoretically balance an elephant, if the mouse had a lever long enough. Or as Archimedes himself similarly declared, in a triumphant tone that reverberates through the millennia, 'Give me a lever and a place to stand, and I can move the earth.'[68]

Archimedes did not invent the lever, but he did something almost as momentous: he outlined a series of logical propositions that, if their implications are followed step-wise, demonstrated (or 'proved') why it works. Unlike another ancient proof that might have been formulated by Euclid (*c.* 300 BCE) and might have been earlier, Archimedes' took a sidestep to what has become a familiar concept today: centre of gravity.[69] In everyday language we say that when objects are not oriented on their centre of gravity they become unstable, as, say, we fall down when we lift a heavy object without compensating for the shift in weight, or when we observe that a vehicle with a high centre of gravity has a tendency to roll over. This is actually not so different from the more formal definition of centre of gravity, which stipulates three distinct properties:

1) The centre of gravity of a symmetrical object or group of objects lies at the middle of the object or group.
2) If an object is hung or supported from its centre of gravity, it will be stable.
3) Any symmetrical object or objects can be swapped for any other object or group, as long at the total weight is the same and the centre of gravity lies at the same point.

To this Archimedes adds several 'postulates', which effectively amount to describing the obvious behaviour of levers:

4) Equal weights at equal distances balance each other. If the distance is unequal, they don't balance.

5) If weights balance, and something is added or taken away from one of them, they no longer balance but incline towards the heavier.

6) Any object or group of objects with the same total weight and identical centres of gravity can be substituted for any equal or similar object or group of objects of the same weight and centres of gravity.

It should be noted that all of these properties (with the possible exception of proposition 6) are fairly intuitive and easily understood by anyone with the kind of grasp of practical mechanics that certainly stretched back to prehistory.[70]

'But why bring up centre of gravity?' the casual observer might ask. 'I thought we were talking about levers.' What Archimedes is doing, in fact, is marshalling all these concepts both explicitly and abstractly, in the sense that what he seeks to prove is true of all objects and groups of objects, everywhere. Indeed, he operates, as Thomas Heath observes, almost like a 'great strategist' who 'strikes the final blow' by calling forth 'proposition after proposition the bearing of which is not immediately obvious but which we find infallibly used later on.'[71] Why seemingly digress to the topic of centre of gravity? Here's why, says Archimedes.

Let us envision that idealized lever again, with weights of four units (say, kilograms) and two units respectively, in balance (illus. 7). In accordance with the law of the lever, the lighter object must be twice as far from the fulcrum as the heavier in order to balance it. The centres of gravity of both objects would lie, of course, at their physical centres, given that both are represented by simple symmetrical shapes. But according to proposition 6, either weight can be replaced by a group of lighter ones, as long as they add up to the same total mass and the group has the same centre of gravity. So

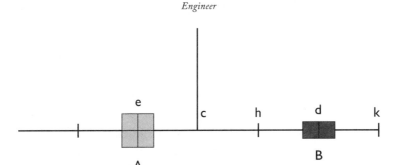

7 Idealized lever with two different weights in equilibrium.
Respective centres of gravity are at e and d.

we can replace the 4-kilogram (9 lb) object with four 1-kilogram
(2.2 lb) objects, and the 2-kilogram (4½ lb) one with two, arrang-
ing both groups symmetrically around the original centre of gravity
of each (illus. 8).

The result is a group of identical weights arranged over the
length of the lever, with the *centre of gravity of all six precisely at
the fulcrum.* According to proposition 2, the grouping must therefore be balanced. Voilà, Archimedes has proven why the law of the
lever must be true. Indeed, he has not only proved it, but done so
in a way that is manifestly obvious.

The proof attributed to Euclid is known only from an Arabic
translation, and may be much older than Euclid himself. It depends
on a purely geometric argument that imagines extending the lever
into a set of two conjoined polygons. Details aside, the Euclidean

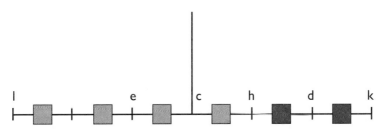

8 Idealized lever with weights in illus. 7 replaced by equal subunits,
distributed around the centres of gravity of the original weights (e and d).
The overall centre of gravity is at c, the fulcrum.

proof is sound, but is not remotely as elegant as Archimedes', and its general applicability is nowhere near as clear as Archimedes' train of equal weights. By taking the reader on a seeming digression into centre of gravity, Archimedes, in effect, sneaks up on a superior solution from a direction most of his readers would not have anticipated. Indeed, given how Archimedes liked to 'tease' his contemporaries, sometimes posing questions in one letter and only divulging his solutions in later ones, it is easy to imagine him enjoying their befuddlement at this indirect approach.

His demonstration that a single person can move a fully laden ship did not employ a simple lever but a system of compound pulleys. The connection between the two is that, in fact, a pulley is functionally equivalent to a lever, with its axis akin to the fulcrum and lengths of rope the lever's 'arms'. Similar is true of gears: a gear wheel with a large diameter can drive a smaller adjoining wheel with greater force, because the hub of the gear is the fulcrum, and the radius of the gear is akin to the length of a lever's arm. (A geartrain can, in a sense, be understood as a chain of rotary levers.) All of which is to say that all the manifestations of Archimedes' engineering – from the pulleys that pulled a ship to the catapults that launched stones to the gears that moved the heavenly bodies in his planetaria – stemmed from the same basic mechanical principle.

Heat Ray

If we are to properly appreciate the magnitude of Archimedes' legacy, it is also important to acknowledge what he did not do. Legends that tell of how he invented (a) the screw pump, (b) gunpowder artillery and (c) the lever itself are still as astonishingly common as they are (a) unlikely, (b) plainly incorrect and (c) downright preposterous. That such inventions, in essence, adhered to his legend is testimony to the almost god-like heights to which his reputation for mechanical invention rose over the centuries.

To take a more recent historical analogy, Benjamin Franklin was indeed a gifted inventor who originated the lightning rod, bifocals, the urinary catheter, an improved wood-burning stove and even, though I am sceptical of this, swim flippers. But the nonsensical notions that Franklin 'discovered electricity' or even invented it are surprisingly common. (If we do an Internet search of the question 'did Benjamin Franklin . . .?', the terms 'invent electricity' and 'discover electricity' are still Google's first suggestions.)

The notion that Archimedes used mirrors to burn Roman ships during the siege of Syracuse is similarly fanciful. That he burned them is certainly possible and in fact likely – the use of burning projectiles such as arrows, pots of flammable materials and flaming shot were well within the technological capabilities of his time. Use of flaming arrows by the Assyrians is attested as early as the eighth century BCE; in the fourth century BCE burning oil, sand and pitch were used against the besieging armies of Alexander the Great at Tyre, among innumerable other historical examples.

And yet, curiously, none of the primary ancient sources for the Syracuse siege (Polybius, Livy and Plutarch) mentions the use of fire against the Romans, let alone burning mirrors. This may simply be because Archimedes' mechanical defences were so remarkable that, by comparison, more conventional weapons simply were not worth mentioning. (Swords, bows and sharp sticks are similarly omitted.) The first unambiguous assertion that Archimedes used reflected sunlight from mirrors as a weapon comes from the pen of Anthemius of Tralles (474–534 CE), who wrote of a 'unanimous tradition that Archimedes used burning mirrors to burn the enemy fleet a bowshot off'.[72] 'Unanimous' or not, that this remarkable technology went unmentioned in any surviving text until some seven centuries after Archimedes' death is suspicious.

The next we hear of it is not until Tzetzes ('The old man constructed some sort of six-angled mirror . . . when the rays, later, were reflected into this, a fearful fiery kindling was lifted to the vessels'[73]) and Joannes Zonaras ('By tilting a kind of mirror toward the Sun he concentrated the Sun's beams on it ... which he directed upon the ships'[74]), writing five and six centuries after Anthemius, respectively – or more than a thousand years after the events they describe. This is not to say that the Byzantine-era sources are necessarily wrong only because they are late. But to say that Archimedes' burning mirrors are not well rooted in the historic record is to put it mildly.

More conclusive is that the heat ray is highly implausible in terms of the evolution of naval warfare. If Archimedes really did manage to use mirrors to burn ships, why did neither the Romans nor anyone else seek to emulate his success? Even at the very apex of the age of wooden warships in the nineteenth century, when knowledge of optics and mirror fabrication were magnitudes better than in Archimedes' time, nobody used mirrors as directed energy weapons. They were used for communication, certainly, and perhaps to dazzle or blind the enemy. But never to set ships on fire.

If we think seriously about what would be involved in igniting a ship with reflected sunlight, we understand why. It is estimated that to focus enough thermal energy on the kind of wooden planks that composed a Roman quinquereme at bowshot distance would have required tracking a rolling, pitching object for a minimum of 30 seconds in rock-steady fashion.[75] As it would be impractical to construct – let alone mount or aim – a single, huge mirror, a series of smaller ones (six? ten? more?) would have had to track a moving ship, all of them focusing in coordinated, sustained fashion on exactly the same spot. This would have been in the heat of battle, with the Romans most likely shooting back. Thirty seconds, again, would have been the minimum: if the ships happened to be wet, which seems possible, and if a cooling wind were blowing, even longer exposure would have been necessary.

Even if they did manage to start a fire, countermeasures would have been easy. There would have been plenty of seawater around to smother any blaze. Or the Romans could have preemptively wetted down their hulls and masts to make it harder to ignite them. (That Archimedes set their sails on fire, instead of the hulls, is unlikely because ancient oared warships furled their sails during combat manoeuvres.) Or the fleet could simply have attacked when it was cloudy, or when the Sun was not in the right position to use as a weapon.

There have been a number of modern attempts to 'recreate' Archimedes' mirror weapon, beginning with the Comte de Buffon in the eighteenth century and as recently as two episodes of the television show *MythBusters* in 2004 and 2006.[76] Buffon reported success with 128 plain glass mirrors; the *MythBusters* team repeatedly fell short and declared the legend 'busted'.[77] None of these attempts resembled real battlefield conditions. Buffon declared victory over a fir tree – hardly a good analogue for a moving Roman ship. Other attempts succeeded in burning plywood models of ships, or targets pre-treated with flammable materials, at closer than a bow-shot, or bone-dry; some utilized modern glass reflectors instead of metal ones true to the period. None properly recreated what Anthemius or Tzetzes describe.

The legend of the burning mirrors must also be evaluated in terms of what alternatives were available. Again, flaming arrows and other projectiles were already proven technology at the time, and may have been more effective still with improved ballistic machines devised by Archimedes. When fire was decisively deployed during a naval siege, most notably by the Byzantines against Arab fleets during the seventh and eighth centuries CE, it was using a chemical substance that was sprayed at the enemy through nozzles, not mirrors.

So is there nothing about this legend that is rooted in fact? One imagines that Archimedes could have used mirrors to disrupt attacks by blinding the enemy, or perhaps, though less plausibly, used focused sunlight to ignite anchored barges filled with highly flammable materials, in the hope that the Roman formations would be disrupted by or collide with the flaming obstacles. But these remain only speculations without any basis in the sources.

There is some evidence that Archimedes did, in fact, write a book on the properties of mirrors ('catoptrics') that mentioned burning things. Apuleius of Madauros (*c.* 125–*c.* 170 CE) reports in his *Apologia* that phenomena of reflection, prismatic effects and 'kindling' of tinder were among 'sundry other phenomena treated in a monumental volume by Archimedes of Syracuse, a man who showed extraordinary and unique subtlety in all branches of geometry, but was perhaps particularly remarkable for his frequent and attentive inspection of mirrors'.[78] Given how remarkable the story is of using burning mirrors against Roman ships, it is therefore strange that Apuleius doesn't mention it. Unless, of course, the legend had not been invented yet.

Of course, a miscellany of conjurers' tricks for making fires was devised over the centuries. One in particular, called 'automatic fire', was a mixture of sulphur, salt, ash, mulberry resin and quicklime that spontaneously burst into flame upon exposure to sunlight.[79] 'Automatic fire' required no mirrors to ignite, but military applications required it to be applied directly to enemy ships, which of course would not have been possible against Marcellus' fleet.

In his thorough assessment of the burning mirrors legend, D. L. Simms concludes it as simply 'invented out of someone's head'.[80] We might be more charitable in calling it a confection of presumptions and attitudes, seasoned with a dash of fact and leavened by frank admiration for the genius of Archimedes. To ancient and medieval minds, the idea of inevitable 'progress' was alien: anything people of their time could accomplish was assumed to be within the capabilities of the giants of the past. If their descendants in Constantinople found a way to incinerate an Arab fleet in the seventh century, the foremost of ancient Greek savants must have had the power to do the same. If sunlight could be used to ignite fires, and if Archimedes wrote a treatise on mirrors, and mentioned burning things with them, and he was a genius, then we begin to see that elements of the legend were readily at hand. All that was required was for someone to put them together.

The Golden Crown Affair

If people know anything about Archimedes, it is probably the incident reported by a Roman some two hundred years after the scientist's death.[81] As Vitruvius was not a historian but an engineer, the truth of his version of the story has long been a target for revisionist criticism – most notably by Galileo – continuing to today (it is a 'nice but silly story', scoffs one of Archimedes' leading contemporary translators[82]). While some of that criticism seems justified, a lot of the backlash seems driven not by the story's implausibility, but by its very appeal.

According to Vitruvius, shortly after Hieron ascended the throne in Syracuse he commissioned an offering to the gods in the form of a golden crown. A certain amount of gold was delivered to the contractor, and when the finished product came back its weight matched the original supply exactly. But at some point suspicions arose that some of the gold had been replaced with silver. Vitruvius doesn't say where these suspicions came from, but this kind of skimming from public resources seems to have been a common accusation levelled at artisans. Phidias (490–430 BCE), an Athenian widely regarded by the ancients themselves as the finest sculptor of his time, was famously also charged with pilfering gold (he was acquitted but died in prison on another charge).[83]

Hieron therefore turned to Archimedes, who, if he wasn't serving officially as court scientist, performed as such here. This prompts the obvious first question: why was he consulted in the first place? After all, the craft of telling precious metal from base – or gold from silver – was certainly well developed long before the

third century BCE. One cannot imagine markets that accept pay-
ment in coins operating without some techniques in common use
for checking debased or counterfeit metal. (Indeed, inscriptions
recovered from fourth-century BCE Athens refer to state-sponsored
evaluators mandated at the markets, with a fifty-lash punishment
for testers who abandoned their posts![84]) Something of the reverse
is also attested by the second century BCE but certainly existed far
earlier: recipes for 'making' gold out of base metals.[85] In practice
this amounted to making alloys that sort of *looked* like gold, at
least in colour.

Archimedes' involvement might be explained by the particular
nature of the crown itself, which was different from how we usually
imagine a crown today. It was more likely a fine golden wreath, a
vegetal sculpture of great delicacy. Though Vitruvius doesn't say
so explicitly, Hieron must have specified that the crown be tested
for its gold content non-destructively, with no part of it removed
or deformed. That said, if some tiny piece of such a crown (like
one twig or leaflet of the wreath masterpiece shown here) was
removed, it is hard to imagine more than one eye in a thousand
being able to tell the difference.

The condition that the crown could not be directly sampled is
often attributed to it being a temple dedication, and so removing
even a small piece of it for testing amounted to 'short-changing' a
god.[86] But neither Vitruvius nor Plutarch affirmatively declare that
the crown had been formally dedicated before Archimedes examined it. Nor is it obvious why a suspect crown would be dedicated
in the first place. Would a god not also be offended by the gift of an
adulterated crown, even one given in ignorance? In *On Divination*,
Cicero reports that Hannibal bored into a column at Juno's temple
at Lacinium to determine if it was solid gold or plated. It was solid,
but Hannibal's research earned him a rebuke from the goddess,
who warned him not to take the entire column at 'the loss of his
good eye'. Hannibal took the hint and appeased Juno by gifting her

9 Gold wreath of olive leaves, *c.* 330–300 BCE.

with the image of a calf sculpted out of bits of gold from his core sample. Yet it was not the sampling of the column that offended the goddess, but the prospect of Hannibal stealing the whole thing. Juno, moreover, seemed more than willing to accept a token of compensation for the insult.[87]

If we look beyond the dubious short-changed-god/dedication issue, the crown problem actually starts to feel like a kind of intellectual game popular among Hellenistic-era mathematicians.[88] Testing a crown accurately without sacrificing any part of it starts to resemble other Archimedean puzzles, like counting the Cattle of the Sun given only the proportions of different colours in the herd. Assuming somewhat artificial conditions, what might have been straightforward tasks (weighing the crown, counting the herd) become devilishly hard problems, demanding out-of-the-box thinking for their solution.

Archimedes' leap out of this particular box is the best-known anecdote about him. Vitruvius writes:

[He] happened to go to the bath, and on getting into a tub observed that the more his body sank into it the more water ran out of the tub. As this pointed out the way to explain the case in question, without a moment's delay, and transported with joy, he jumped out of the tub and rushed home naked, crying with a loud voice that he had found what he was seeking ['Eureka!'].

This story has since become one of a select few historical archetypes of abrupt scientific insight, like the apple falling on Newton's head. What Archimedes supposedly realized here was one of the principles of static buoyancy: objects submerged in water displace it according to their volumes, not their mass. Such objects, moreover, are subject to an upward (buoyant) force exactly equal to the amount of water they displace. The more deeply Archimedes' body settled into the tub, the more water sloshed over the rim, and the greater force supported him. This is an abstract way of describing what is intuitively obvious. A solid ball of steel weighing 10,000 tons dropped in the ocean would sink straight to the bottom; the exact same mass in the form of a submarine would not sink, because the less dense, hollow vessel displaces more than 10,000 tons of water.

How did this realization help Archimedes test Hieron's crown? In essence, the displacement test gave him a way to measure, in a non-destructive manner, the volume (and with its weight, a way to calculate the density) of a highly irregular object. The gold in the crown and a lump of equivalent weight in pure gold should have identical density (specifically, 19.3 grams per cubic centimetre), and therefore – notwithstanding the crown's far more complex shape – identical volume. Conversely, a crown alloyed with silver (10.5 g/cc) or copper (9 g/cc) would be less dense, and therefore would need to be physically bulkier to weigh the same as the sample of gold.

Distinguishing between pure and adulterated cases would therefore be a simple matter of plunging the crown and a gold sample of equal weight into water. If the former causes more water to spill over the brim – if it displaces more water than the latter – its volume must be larger, and its density correspondingly less. Apparently this is exactly what Archimedes found: 'reasoning from the fact that more water was lost in the case of the crown than in that of the mass', relates Vitruvius, 'he detected the mixing of silver with the gold, and made the theft of the contractor perfectly clear.' He gives no word on the fate of the artisan with the sticky fingers.

This is a neat story, and a bit touching given Archimedes' child-like excitement in solving the puzzle. Too neat and too touching for some, perhaps: Galileo, in his first published scientific treatise, *La bilancetta* (The Little Balance, 1586), declared that it could not have happened the way Vitruvius described. The amount of water displaced respectively from an ordinary bowl of water by the crown and the gold sample would be, according to Galileo, so small as to be indistinguishable. In other words, he argued that Archimedes lacked the means to measure water in amounts minute enough to be diagnostic.

What he probably did instead, reasoned Galileo, was rig up a way to measure the buoyant force of the crown and gold sample directly, by placing them on a scale that was in turn immersed in water. If the crown side of the scale rose relative to the sample side, the crown must be less dense, and therefore adulterated with some other metal. Using the known technology of his time, Archimedes could have made such a 'hydrostatic balance' as sensitive as required.

This approach was actually presaged by the Latin grammarian Remus Favinus in his poem *Carmen de ponderibus et mensuris* (Song of Weights and Measures) of around 400 CE. Favinus like-wise spoke of a balance immersed in water that could tell pure gold from gold adulterated with silver.[89] Whether or not Galileo derived his inspiration from Favinus, his argument has convinced some.[90] And yet it has a few problems of its own.

First, while it is true that the amount of displaced water from an ordinary bowl would be very small in both cases, Vitruvius says nothing about the shape of the vessel Archimedes used in his test. The water level of a container with a low surface-to-volume ratio – say, one shaped more like a narrow cylinder – would more clearly show the difference in displacement, for the same reason that the level of water poured into a high, narrow glass rises more obviously than the exact same amount of water poured into a shallow, wide one. That is why we use a graduated cylinder to measure volumes of liquids in chemistry labs, not a graduated finger-bowl.

How much trouble would it have been for Archimedes to procure a narrow cylindrical vessel for his test? It is hard to say, but certainly no more trouble than devising Galileo's fancy hydrostatic balance, festooned (as he describes) with adjustable copper wires for precise calibration. Alas, La bilancetta seems more about the 22-year-old Galileo demonstrating his own ingenuity than about Archimedes'.

Second, water clocks and other fluid-driven devices, like water organs, are copiously attested starting in the Hellenistic period. Some of these clocks kept time well enough to be useful at night, when sundials were obviously not useable. A constant-flow water valve was invented by Ktesibius of Alexandria, an exact contemporary of Archimedes.[91] Such devices, if they kept time even moderately well, inevitably demanded precise regulation of relatively small amounts of water. Archimedes himself wrote a treatise, lost now but mentioned in Arab sources, on the principles of water clocks, and built a few himself.[92] One of them was reportedly so ingenious that it sounded the hours by means of a mechanical raven dropping marbles on a metal tray. All this suggests that any pronouncements on the level of precision of ancient engineers in measuring the flow of water are premature, to say the least.

Third, if Archimedes thought of the crown challenge as, in essence, a problem of measuring the volume of an irregular object, then his solution (and exuberant reaction to it) is very much in the spirit of his abstract geometric work. An enduring project in ancient Greek mathematics lay in finding ways to measure things that are relatively complicated (circles, spheres, cylinders, parabolic segments and so on) in terms of things that are simple (triangles, squares). This was what the phrase 'to square the circle' meant. We will revisit this theme below, but for now suffice it to say that Archimedes' fundamental technique was to break complex objects down into very small regular ones that, like tiny measuring sticks, can be added up to yield something very close to the total. In the same way that tiny mosaic tiles can fill up a circular frame more efficiently than big ones, the smaller the measuring sticks become, the better they collectively fill an irregular space. As they approached infinitely small, Archimedes could add them up to get as close to the total complex area or volume as he wished.

This is likely what Archimedes really meant when he cried 'Eureka!' As he sank into his tub, he perceived that the water he displaced was equal to the volume of his body he had submerged, not his weight. It didn't matter if the submerged object was simple or complex, because the components of water are so infinitesimal they fill every possible bump and crevice of any conceivable object, even one as irregular as a human body – or a crown. In the same way Archimedes could measure the area of a circle by filling it in with smaller and smaller triangles, he could precisely measure the volume of the crown by letting it displace the constituent particles of water ('atoms' to the ancient Greeks, 'molecules' to chemists today) that approach infinity in their smallness.

Plutarch declared that Archimedes valued the offspring of his abstract research over the children of his practical pursuits. He might have been right. But by conceiving of the crown problem this way we see that it is not silly at all, but shows how the abstract

and the practical are like conjoined twins, sharing a way of thinking that sustains both. It is a theme we will encounter again, when
we consider what might be his most radical work, the *Method of
Mechanical Theorems*.

One further implication of the crown story deserves comment.
This focuses not so much on the significance of what Archimedes
realized in his bath, which critics are probably justified in saying
was not up to genius standards. Insofar as the 'running in the
street naked' part is true, what is interesting is not whether he was
buck-naked or only lightly clad, but that Archimedes did not just
sit back and privately relish his insight. He jumped up and celebrated in the streets. He cried out so everybody around him knew
of his achievement. He cried 'Eureka!' repeatedly at passersby. He
engaged in a public display.

This underscores that Archimedes was hardly some kind of
cloistered philosopher, sustaining himself on the rarefied manna
of rational progress. He was a public intellectual. In this regard,
Vitruvius' story has the ring of truth, because it accords well with
other details of Archimedes' career. For instance, consider him
single-handedly launching a full-size ship from its berth on land,
utilizing a system of compound pulleys of his design. This was
done in the presence of King Hieron and other onlookers, including a full complement of passengers on board.[93] If this display
had failed, it would have failed spectacularly. It was nothing less
than theatre, with Archimedes coming off as a kind of scientific
impresario.

A similar drive for recognition appears to motivate his correspondence with his peers. Upon working out his proofs,
Archimedes would issue open challenges, sharing the theorems he
had proved and inviting others to work out their own independent
solutions (a task made easier, in fact, by Archimedes telling them
in advance that they were soluble). But in a letter sent to Dositheus,
he complains that no one – 'not … a single person' – has attempted

to uncover proofs to the theorems he mooted to his diligent but sadly deceased friend Conon. He divulges, moreover, that two of the theorems he sent are actually 'poisoned', having no possible proofs. In this way, if some fraudster claimed a proof but declined to provide it, Archimedes could immediately declare their dishonesty, 'by promising to find solutions to impossible theorems'. It is hard to read any of this – the complaints that no one is up to replicating his work, the recourse to insurance against spurious claims – without feeling the intensity of Archimedes' thirst for acclaim, not just from kings but from the wider community of mathematicians.[94]

A drive not just for contemporary but eternal fame is discernible in his correspondence with Eratosthenes, chief librarian at the Great Library at Alexandria. In sharing a copy of his *Method*, Archimedes was not only challenging the polymath Eratosthenes to recognize his ingenuity. He also fully expected Eratosthenes to deposit the book in the library for the benefit of future generations:

> I have decided to write down and make known the method partly because I have already spoken of it, so that no one would think that I was uttering idle talk, and partly in the conviction that it would be of no small use for mathematics; for I suppose that there will be some among present or future individuals who will discover by the method here set forth still other theorems which have not yet occurred to us.

This is a man who basked in appreciation from his contemporaries, valued his reputation for integrity, brooked no charge of 'idle talk' about his accomplishments and sought to project a legacy beyond his lifetime. This is far indeed from a cloistered, aloof cartoon figure too disengaged from his environment to hear his city fall – or the approaching footsteps of his murderer.

Titanic

The giantism embodied in Archimedes' war machines extended to other endeavours. In his *Deipnosophistae* (Dinner Experts/Gastronomers), a third-century CE miscellany of learned table-talk, Athenaeus of Naucratis describes a massive ship that was constructed for Hieron with vital help from Archimedes. The *Syracusia* was some 75 metres (246 ft) long with a beam that stretched 20 metres (65 ft), and is estimated from Athenaeus' detailed description to have displaced some 4,000 to 5,000 tonnes at full load.[95] This is truly enormous by ancient standards: a typical merchant vessel of the time, such as the Kyrenia ship recovered off the coast of Cyprus in 1967, displaced only 28 tonnes. To build her, enough wood was harvested from the slopes of Mt Etna for sixty triremes. She would have been two or three times as heavy as the *Isis*, one of the big grain ships used to feed the Roman Empire four centuries later.[96] She would have been longer and heavier than HMS *Victory*, Nelson's 104-gun flagship at Trafalgar. She would have been 50 per cent bigger than SS *Great Western*, the largest passenger ship in the world in 1838 and the first paddle-driven steamship to cross the Atlantic. To sail, defend and maintain her would have required a crew comparable in size to a Second World War fleet battleship.[97]

Though the *Syracusia* was simultaneously a warship, a cargo vessel and a cruise ship, its primary purpose was to serve as an advertisement of Hieron's wealth. The pure stupefying excess of its appointments makes it worth quoting Athenaeus at length:

> And the vessel was constructed with twenty banks of oars, and three entrances ... And all these rooms had floors composed of mosaic work, of all kinds of stones tessellated. And on this mosaic the whole story of the Iliad was depicted in a marvellous manner. And in all the furniture and the ceilings

and the doors everything was executed and finished in the same admirable manner. And along the uppermost passage was a gymnasium and walks, having their appointments in all respects corresponding to the size of the vessel. And in them were gardens of all sorts of most wonderful beauty, enriched with all sorts of plants, and shaded by roofs of lead or tiles. And besides this there were tents roofed with boughs of white ivy and of the vine, the roots of which derived their moisture from casks full of earth, and were watered in the same manner as the gardens. And the tents themselves helped to shadow the walks. And next to these things was a temple devoted to Venus, containing three couches, with a floor of agate and other most beautiful stones, of every sort which the island afforded. And its walls and its roof were made of cypress-wood, and its doors of ivory and citron-wood. And it was furnished in the most exquisite manner with pictures and statues, and with goblets and vases of every form and shape imaginable…

And there was also a bath-room, capable of containing three couches, having three brazen vessels for holding hot water, and a bath containing five measures of water, beautifully variegated with Tauromenian marble… And besides all this there were ten stalls for horses on each side of the walls; and by them the fodder for the horses was kept, and the arms and furniture of the horsemen and of the boys. There was also a cistern near the head of the ship, carefully shut, and containing two thousand measures of water, made of beams closely compacted with pitch and canvass. And next to the cistern there was a large water-tight well for fish, made so with beams of wood and lead. And it was kept full of sea-water, and great numbers of fish were kept in it… And the whole ship was adorned with suitable pictures.[98]

It is hard to say whether Archimedes had anything to do with designing the crew accommodations, gymnasium, Temple of Venus, hot-and-cold-water marble bathrooms, horse stable, gardens or on-board fish farm. The ship did bristle with defensive weapons, however, and in this his hand is obvious:

> And in the vessel were eight towers of a size proportioned to the burden of the ship, two at the stem, and as many at the head, and the rest in the middle of the ship. And to each of these were fastened two large beams, or yards, from which port-holes were fixed, through which stones were let down upon any enemy who might come against the ship. And on each of the towers stood four young men fully armed, and two archers. And the whole of the interior of the towers was full of stones and darts. And a wall, having buttresses and decks, ran all through the ship, supported on trestles; and on these decks was placed a catapult, which hurled a stone weighing three talents, and an arrow twelve cubits long. And this engine was devised and made by Archimedes; and it could throw every arrow a furlong.

These sound very much like the measures Archimedes designed for the defence of the city itself. He was also responsible for one of the key features that made the *Syracusia* even conceivable: as such a large wooden hull would have leaked like a sieve, the efficiency of the ship's pumps was of existential importance. But according to Athenaeus, 'the hold, although of a most enormous depth, was *pumped out by one man,* by means of a pulley, by an engine which was the contrivance of Archimedes' (emphasis added). To repeat: by means of a mechanism designed by Archimedes, the hold of a vessel bigger than an eighteenth-century ship of the line was kept dry by one man.

Seaworthy in port is not the same as seaworthy on the waves, of course. The *Syracusia* made a single long-distance voyage when Hieron, as another expression of soft power, gifted it to King Ptolemy III of Egypt, along with a hold full of grain and salted fish to relieve a famine there. No larger vessel had plied the seas since Noah, and none bigger would sail for more than 2,000 years.

One imagines the impression the vessel must have made as she lumbered into the harbour of Alexandria, forcing smaller vessels to scatter before her. The *Syracusia*'s appearance inspired the (possibly mythical) poet Archimelus to celebrate her in verse:

Surely it equals Ætna in its height,
Or any isle which rises from the sea
Where the Ægean wave entwined foams
Amid the Cyclades; on either side
Its breadth is equal, and its walls alike.
Sure 'twas the giants' work, who hoped to reach
By such vast ladder to the heights of heaven.
Its topmast reaches to the stars; and hides
Its mighty bulwarks 'mid the endless clouds.

Is there any doubt that Archimedes' colleague and correspondent Eratosthenes, head of the Great Library, would have gone down to the port to marvel at her?

If imitation is the sincerest form of flattery, then Hieron must have been flattered indeed by Ptolemy's response to his monumental gift. The latter went on to commission an even bigger vessel, even more sumptuously equipped, that was almost twice as long and boasted forty banks of oars. Ptolemy's leviathan was just a floating showpiece, however, so dangerous to actually sail that there is no record of her ever having left port.[99]

With most of their warships only one-sixtieth the displacement of the *Syracusia*, even veteran admirals in Hieron's court must have

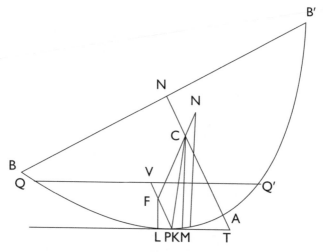

10 Diagram based on Proposition 2 of the second book *On Floating Bodies*. The proof shows the conditions under which a paraboloid placed in fluid (surface at Q-Q') will return to a state of equilibrium if inclined.

expected it to simply roll over and sink. In addition to his contributions as engineer, Archimedes would have dispelled this fear in his two books *On Floating Bodies*. Here, in a series of propositions that brilliantly build on each other, he outlines a geometric theory of hydrostatics that proves the conditions under which parabolic sections would or would not be stable when in, on or immersed in a fluid. These parabolic sections are, of course, very much like the profiles of ships' hulls – of whatever size.

Like his famous dictum about levers, Archimedes might easily have declared, 'Give me a hull large enough, and I'll make the Moon float.' Here, yet again, we see how the line between theory and practice was blurred in treatises that appear, on the surface, to be purely abstract in subject.

The Dial of Destiny

The National Archaeological Museum in Athens is full of beautiful objects, but the ugliest is arguably the most significant. Coming upon the Antikythera Mechanism in the exhibition hall, the casual observer encounters fragments of what appears to be the post-apocalyptic remains of a modern clock. Recovered from a shipwreck off the coast of the Greek island of Antikythera in 1901, covered with sickly green concretions from 2,000 years at the bottom of the Mediterranean, the pieces are fragmentary and hard for the layperson to interpret. In the decades immediately after its recovery, the museum displayed it fitfully, and rarely with all the major fragments together. But growing awareness of the significance of the world's first true mechanical computing device has prompted (excuse the expression) a sea change in its visibility. When I first saw it in 2007, the fragments were housed in a single case in the middle of a gallery devoted to other treasures. By 2022 the remains had a room to themselves, with related materials spilling over into one and a half more. The story of the mechanism is told in more depth in my book *Circumference* as well as in several very good book-length treatments.[100] But here we will concentrate on what it might mean for the work and legacy of Archimedes.

In the century or so since its discovery, investigation of the device has gone through a number of phases. The German philologist Albert Rehm deployed what military types call the 'Mark I Eyeball' in his examination of the external surface. He discovered inscriptions referring to concepts the Greeks inherited and refined from those great astronomers the Babylonians. Flat-plane X-ray imagery revealed hidden gear-work in the 1970s, leading physicist Derek J. de Solla Price to the first comprehensive theory of the machine's operation. Advances in our understanding have followed advances in imaging technology, including three-dimensional X-ray tomography and other digital imaging techniques that have allowed investigators to peer inside the corroded pieces and read more of the inscriptions. With this data, teams led by Michael Wright (formerly of the London Science Museum) and film-maker/mathematician Tony Freeth have progressed to what seems to be solid understanding of most of the mechanism's functions – though some mysteries remain.[101]

The mechanism was a mechanical calculating device that allowed the user to simulate the motions of the Sun, the Moon, and all the planets known in antiquity, as well as predict lunar and solar eclipses and certain other cultural events, namely the four Panhellenic games that alternated in a four-year cycle in mainland

11 Fragment A of the Antikythera Mechanism, which was recovered in 1901 from the remains of an ancient shipwreck, as displayed in 2022 at the National Archaeological Museum, Athens.

Greece. After setting the positions of the dials, the device was hand-cranked to, in essence, run time forwards or backwards. Astonishingly, it accurately represented a number of apparently irregular motions, including the way some planets sometimes seem to move backwards in the sky, and the variable evolutions of the Moon. It did all this without necessarily instantiating any particular model of the cosmos, geocentric, heliocentric or otherwise. (In the term used in antiquity, it 'saved the appearance' of what happens in the sky without requiring knowledge of how it happens.) The shoe-box-sized device did all this using a complex train of precision gears otherwise unknown from the period of its construction. Indeed, no device of comparable complexity is known until the fourteenth century CE, on the cusp of the modern mechanical revolution. With some justification, its discovery has been compared to digging up a Buick from medieval Europe.[102]

The design of the device was initially credited to a Greek astronomer in the Roman period, such as Poseidonius (135–*c.* 51 BCE) or Geminus (*c.* 110–40 BCE), both of Rhodes. A Rhodian origin is strongly suspected because the ship carrying the mechanism at least stopped there en route to its intended destination, and because it was a place where the long tradition of Greek scholarship was relatively free to carry on.[103] (The Great Library at Alexandria had by that time declined, after King Ptolemy VIII expelled many intellectuals from the city in 145 BCE.[104])

Recently, however, the name of Archimedes has been raised in connection with the mechanism. Enhanced examination of the inscriptions on the back face revealed the names of months in Greek, which is useful for identifying the origin of the device because different Greek cultural traditions used different calendar terms. Historian Alexander Jones attributed the names to the Doric Greek tradition that included Corinth and her colonies, including Syracuse.[105] In fact, the terms most resemble those used in Tauromenion (now Taormina) in Sicily, a colony founded (technically, re-founded) by Dionysius I of Syracuse in 392 BCE. However, other inscriptions are in the Attic-Ionic dialect used in Athens and the Aegean basin. The inscribed names of recurring events in the sky, such as the solstices, conform best to an observer in the northern hemisphere between the latitudes of 33.3 and 37.0 degrees.[106] This range includes both Rhodes and Syracuse, but not Alexandria. Notwithstanding this confusion, Freeth has drawn connections between the mechanism and Archimedes himself, writing, 'It may well be that the Antikythera Mechanism was based on a design by Archimedes.' Indeed, he goes even further to declare that the 'ingenuity [of the machine] reinforces the idea that the machine was *designed by Archimedes*' (emphasis added).[107] Directly attributing the mechanism to such a famous name has certainly increased popular interest in it. But is the claim justified?

To assess that question, we need a solid understanding of what the evidence can mean and what it cannot. For instance, the geo-graphical origin of month or festival names might tell us about where the device was made, but it might also tell us where it was intended to be used. Based on the number of explicit instructions on the face of the machine, it is likely that it was not made for a pro-fessional astronomer (whatever that meant in the first or second century BCE),[108] but for an educated amateur who needed to be walked through every step of its use. The mechanism is, in a real sense, a consumer product, designed for a very specialized clien-tele. Is it plausible that Archimedes himself, in his spare moments when he wasn't doing high-level geometry and building seagoing leviathans and designing the defence of Syracuse, would have taken part in an overseas trade in luxury accessories?

Archimedes apparently did design and build similar mecha-nisms. A treatise called *On Sphere-Making* is mentioned by Pappus of Alexandria (c. 290–350 CE), which Dijksterhuis concludes 'can hardly have dealt with anything but the manner in which he constructed contrivances such as his planetaria.'[109] Book VIII of

Pappus' *Collection* (*c.* 340) is devoted to mechanical problems, and includes a discussion of the mathematics of linked gears with differing numbers of teeth, including their diameters and speeds of rotation:

> Now let us assume that drum A has 60 teeth, and B has 40 teeth: I mean, let the speed of A be multiplied by the speed of B, so that the number of teeth of drum B is equal to the number of teeth of A. For since the tympanums A and B are attached to each other, as many teeth of the tympanum B will be moved, as many will also be moved from A itself.[110]

Pappus' treatment of gear-trains is little known, and brief, and late, coming some six centuries after Archimedes' death. But it takes on added significance with the discovery of the Antikythera Mechanism, suggesting that Pappus had access to a literature, now almost entirely lost, directly related to principles underlying such complex devices.

The literati offer their testimony too. Ovid (43 BCE–*c.* 17 CE), in his *Fasti*, versifies about a spherical mechanism representing the cosmos, made 'by Syracusan art'.[111] Cicero likewise describes one of these spheres in his *De re publica*, having his character Philus describe a celestial globe,

> on which were delineated the motions of the Sun and Moon and of those five stars which are called wanderers, or, as we might say, rovers, contained more than could be shown on the solid globe, and the invention of Archimedes deserved special admiration because he had thought out a way to represent accurately by a single device for turning the globe those various and divergent movements with their different rates of speed. And when Gallus moved the globe, it was actually true that the Moon was always as

12 Speculative reconstruction of Archimedes' sphere in the Kotsanas Museum
of Ancient Greek Technology, Athens.

many revolutions behind the Sun on the bronze contrivance as would agree with the number of days it was behind it in the sky. Thus the same eclipse of the Sun happened on the globe as would actually happen . . .[112]

Cicero elsewhere refers to a similar machine built by Poseidonius, with whom he personally studied in Rhodes and who he proudly calls a friend.[113] The device, he says, 'at each revolution reproduces the same motions of the Sun, the Moon, and the five planets'. But Archimedes' device so exceeded all others that some 'think that Archimedes did more in imitating the revolutions of the sphere than nature did in producing them'.[114]

In the Kotsanas Museum of Ancient Greek Technology in Athens there is a speculative reconstruction of what Cicero and Ovid describe. The look of the machine is very different from the boxy Antikythera Mechanism. Indeed, it is a far more intuitively elegant device for representing the spherical extension of the heavens.

Did Archimedes design the very device now in the Athens Archaeological Museum? Coins recovered from the wreck indicate the ship sailed no earlier than 85 BCE. Repairs made to the mechanism suggest that it was used for some time before it was lost, but there is no way of knowing how long it was made before the wreck. Looking at the dials on the back face, the device is most accurate if we assume it was calibrated for an eclipse cycle beginning in 205 BCE, or seven years after Archimedes' death. But a calibration date doesn't necessarily prove when it was constructed, any more than if I drew up a modern paper calendar today that started with my birthday and it was thus assumed I put pen to paper in my crib in 1963.

That Archimedes' work on 'sphere-making' *inspired* the calculating devices that followed is plausible. His influence might be compared to that of Alan Turing, who pioneered modern computer science but had nothing immediately to do with the iPhone in your pocket. But – barring future discoveries like an inscription saying 'Archimedes Made Me' – his direct authorship is hard to justify. Historian of science Herbert Bruderer summed it up well: 'If the astronomical calculator had been manufactured by Archimedes during his lifetime, it would have been approximately 150 years old when the ship sank. Such an early production does not seem very plausible.'[115]

Nightfall

After Archimedes' death in 212 BCE there is no record of anyone taking up his mantle in Syracuse, or anywhere else in Sicily. Though it is possible he had assistants or students, it does not appear that he succeeded in replicating himself either as a scientist or engineer, or that he even tried.

Greek mathematics and science carried on with other figures whose works have survived either directly or in references by others. Apollonius of Perge (c. 240–190 BCE) worked in Pergamon and Alexandria, and published a treatise on conic sections that became the standard work on the subject. There are hints that Archimedes himself knew of this younger contemporary, and perhaps engaged in some playful rivalry.[116] The ensuing generation also included Hipparchus of Nicaia (190–120 BCE), who may have been the foremost observational astronomer of classical antiquity, having discovered precession of the equinoxes and laid the foundation for trigonometry. Seleucus of Seleucia (c. 190–c. 150 BCE) was a Babylonian or Babylonian Greek who developed Aristarchus' heliocentric theory of the cosmos and was among the first to correctly explain the tides. We have already had occasion to mention Poseidonius and Geminus of Rhodes. Claudius Ptolemaeus (c. 100–c. 170 CE) devised the geocentric model of the heavens that stood as the standard one in Europe until Copernicus, and was arguably the most widely cited scientist of any until modern times. He also did notable work in geography, music theory and optics. Diophantus of Alexandria (*c.* 200–*c.* 285 CE) did significant foundational work on what we know today as algebra.

Archimedes' contemporaries as an engineer include Philon of Byzantium (*c.* 280–*c.* 220 BCE), who described pneumatic devices, a water mill, the first repeating crossbow and an unspillable inkstand that qualifies as the world's first gimbal. Athenaeus of Seleucia (first century BCE, known as 'Mechanicus') later claimed to have adapted Philon's ink-gimbal to military use for stabilizing large siege engines mounted on ships – an invention truly in the spirit of Archimedes, if it was actually ever used.[117] Heron of Alexandria (*c.* 10–*c.* 70 CE) is perhaps the best-known ancient engineer after Archimedes; his inventions include the first steam-powered 'engine' (strictly speaking, a kind of steam-driven propeller), the first vending machine, a programmable self-propelled vehicle, a self-filling wine cup and an organ powered by wind, among other wonders.[118] There is no record, however, that anybody followed up on the mechanisms Archimedes devised to defend Syracuse. Nobody ever managed (or thought) to attempt to snatch whole ships out of the water again, much less use mirrors to set them on fire.

There was definitely life in Greek science and technology after the death of Archimedes. Still, there is a sense that progress was not what it could have been. This or that figure contributed, to be sure, but advancement seems to have proceeded in deliberate, linear fashion, with innovations and discoveries following each other but not necessarily building momentum. By the first century CE, Pliny the Elder (23–79) could plausibly complain that 'nowadays, in this happy time of peace . . . absolutely nothing is being added to the sum of knowledge as a result of original research.'[119] There is no hedging to his language here (*'omnino nihil'*, 'absolutely nothing'), suggesting that Pliny expected few of his contemporaries would bother to dispute him. Contrast this to the trajectory of science and technology in the modern era, which has accelerated exponentially to the breakneck speed it has today.

There is a large literature on the question of why, despite the evident genius of many Greek and Roman-era scientists and engineers, ancient science didn't go further.[120] True, in an important sense it is an unfair question, given that we know of no iron rule that all complex civilization must inevitably undergo mechanization.[121] To expect so is to normalize our experience, a cardinal sin when trying to make sense of the past in its own terms.

What we identify as science in antiquity can only be understood in a socioeconomic context that was very different to our own. By Hellenistic times, notes historian Peter Green, 'the main aim of wealthy landowners was not so much to make wealth as to spend it.' Profit was not ploughed back into innovations that drove increasing productivity, but mostly invested back into land.[122] The moral virtue of constant wealth acquisition for its own sake, which we might objectively suspect is a kind of madness, had not yet assumed the primacy it did during the early modern period. It is also broadly true that the influence of the merchant classes, and the imperative to support the function of markets, were not as compelling as they came to be later. Though commerce affected the politics of Rome, and politics the commerce of later mercantile powers like Venice, the Netherlands and England, there was certainly a quantitative difference between them.

The cultural context was likewise far different. Typical of certain philosophic attitudes towards so-called 'banausic' (that is, 'material' or 'utilitarian') innovation was the Roman Stoic philosopher and dramatist Seneca (4 BCE–65 CE), who, in describing the nature of true wisdom, argues that mere cleverness is not wisdom:

In these our own times, which man, pray, do you deem the wiser – the one who invents a process for spraying saffron perfumes to a tremendous height from hidden pipes, who fills or empties canals by a sudden rush of waters, who so cleverly constructs a dining-room with a ceiling of movable panels ... or the one who proves to others, as well as to himself, that nature has laid upon us no stern and difficult law when she tells us that we can live without the marble-cutter and the engineer, that we can clothe ourselves without traffic in silk fabrics, that we can have everything that is indispensable to our use, provided only that we are content with what the earth has placed on its surface?'[123]

'It is my opinion that the wise man has not withdrawn himself from these [practical] arts,' Seneca goes on, 'but that he never took them up at all.'[124] Notwithstanding the alleged humbleness of his life-style, one wonders what Archimedes would have said about the wisdom of never taking up engineering at all.

Of course, it is easy to see Seneca's noble primitivism as highly convenient for an elite like himself, who had plenty of slaves at his disposal to give him the leisure to write moralizing letters extolling independence from convenience. (Tacitus quotes a contemporary critic, 'What branch of learning, what philosophical school, won Seneca three hundred million sesterces during four years of imperial friendship?'[125]) But his attitude nevertheless had a deep pedigree among those in the upper classes, Greek and Roman. The philosopher Epicurus (341–270 BCE) likewise argues that 'we must not suppose that any other object is to be gained from the knowledge of the phenomena of the sky ... than peace of mind and a sure confidence.'[126]

As the purpose of science was not material advancement but peace of mind, ancient science was in direct competition with religion and philosophy for the attention of the era's best intellects. By Archimedes' time, the focus of philosophical inquiry in Athens had long since moved on from mathematics/physical science.[127] The rising role of Christianity later, both in actively suppressing pagan rationalism and passively depriving it of institutional oxygen, cannot be ignored.[128] A general malaise, a certain disenchantment with rational inquiry, became palpable in late antiquity, as the lack of a strong experimental component made many fundamental debates seem unresolvable and therefore, in the worst sense of the word, 'academic'.[129] Even as early at the first century BCE, Cicero hinted that the kind of theoretical research done by Archimedes was associated more closely with the defeated Greeks, whose glory lay in the past. The future, Cicero's rhetoric implied, would hinge more on Roman virtues like statecraft, rhetoric and morals.[130]

Reviel Netz, in a recent history of ancient Greek mathematics, offers an even more socially mediated explanation: preoccupation with certain classes of problems tended to rise and fall in generational cycles. Interest usually begins with some kind of sage (Pythagoras, Thales, Socrates and so on) who makes momentous pronouncements to his circle of followers (for example, 'All is number') but writes nothing down. The next generation engages with those big ideas, developing them in books and perhaps making a name by challenging them. After that very often comes . . . *nothing*. Once the low-hanging fruit is collected, collective attention tends to shift to some other class of problem, one that offers more opportunity to establish independent status. The cycle begins anew. While most of Netz's examples lie in the realm of metaphysics, there seems to be no inherent reason why the theory cannot apply to the study of plain old physics too. As we suggest above, Archimedes' own motives in engineering his spheres and weapons may have had a lot to do with winning a name for himself. But after his success, and that of others like Heron, the cycles they started petered out, as the best minds sought advancement doing something else.[131]

Netz's hypothesis is interesting and seems to fit the patchy historiographic record. Yet it does have the ring of a description posing as an explanation. The pattern of most scientific inquiry, after all, is one of solutions generating more questions, which tend to lead to advancement and more interesting questions. The pattern appears to be self-perpetuating – except among the Greeks, where it notably was not. Indeed, in almost no field can it be said that they harvested all the low-hanging fruit. So it is still necessary to appeal to other explanations, including lack of institutional support, philosophic ennui and Christianity, to understand why those succeeding generations largely gave up on science.

Archimedes' fame as a 'machinist' never seems to have waned. Indeed, it seemed only to grow as stories became attached to his legend, such as 'inventing' the screw pump and incinerating Roman ships with mirrors.[132] Yet his purely abstract works came to be represented poorly in the libraries of late antiquity. Ironically, his challenging analytic style may also have contributed to this. It is a factor we will have occasion to discuss next, as we turn to his legacy as a pure mathematician.

2

Mathematician

For most of classical antiquity, the principal technology for publishing and consuming books was the scroll (in ancient Greek, τόμος; in Latin, *volumen* – whence our English words 'tome' and 'volume').[1] Made of sheets of split and flattened stalks of Egyptian papyrus that were glued together into rolls, the scroll had certain advantages that help explain its long tenure. Presenting what was essentially a long connected string of text, it was excellent for consuming written works in continuous fashion.[2] The oral performance of poetry or history, important in a society with limited literacy, did not require the pauses and reorientations obliged by flipping pages. Notwithstanding how expensive papyrus became, rolls were relatively cheap, durable and transportable. Anyone who was aware of the works of Archimedes in the latter Hellenistic and most of the Roman period would have read him (and of him) in scrolls.

The trouble is, though stories about Archimedes himself were always well known, his mathematical and mechanical works were not necessarily the most popular. What later references we have to them are scattered and scanty: a mention in a discussion of conic sections in a work by Diocles, who lived soon after Archimedes;[3] an encomium in the first century CE by Heron of Alexandria in the Preamble of his *Metrica*, regarding the volume and surface area of an enclosed sphere; a reference by Theon of Alexandria (335–405 and father of the famous Hypatia) to Archimedes' lost *Catoptrica*.[4]

According to Eutocius of Ascalon, Diocles and Dionysodorus of Caunus attempted to reconstruct one piece of his work, a proof from *On the Sphere and Cylinder*, that was already lost by the second century BCE. By 500 CE, only a handful of his works (*Sphere and Cylinder*, *Measurement of a Circle* and *Equilibrium of Planes*) were 'generally known'.[5] Dijksterhuis observes, while 'people soon began to study the more elementary works . . . the profounder investigations fell more or less into oblivion'.[6]

The tension inherent in this – being one of the most renowned minds of his era, yet little read – is often blamed on his contemporaries' trouble in understanding him. Even some modern mathematicians, perfectly comfortable with concepts inconceivable to ancient minds, have trouble wrapping their heads around Archimedes' *Quadrature of the Parabola*.[7] To read Archimedes is to follow someone who revels in spinning intricate skeins of argument that depend on simultaneously holding multiple propositions in mind. Very often that effort is spent trying to prove the *opposite* of what he promises to show, and by uncovering some key contradiction or inconsistency, a double negative. Propositions seem to come out of nowhere, with little apparent motivation, until their relevance is dramatically sprung later. After leading us out of those labyrinths, he subjects us to head-spinning turns that lead us, dazed and exhausted, to conclusions as grand as sun-drenched temples.

Not for nothing does one of his modern translators describe the 'intricacy and surprise' of his proofs, conjoined with an 'inherent simplicity' that belies their apparent complexity. 'The intricacy', writes historian of ancient mathematics Reviel Netz, 'arises, in a sense, from the simplicity . . . The mathematical elegance of the work goes hand-in-hand with its surprise and suspense.'[8] At a time when science was about attaining 'peace of mind', consuming such intricate, 'suspenseful' works became akin to, as one of Archimedes' treatises came to be called, *Stomachion* – a 'bone fight'. Needless to say, the audience for such challenging material was very limited to begin with.

This situation was further complicated by the fact that, until relatively late, Archimedes' works were not presented conveniently in collected volumes. They existed originally in scattered form, in letters sent to and preserved by his peers. Those attempting to build on his work might have access to only some of what he produced, or only imperfect versions based on haphazard copying. That copying was, in many cases, done by scribes who may have had no understanding of the material they were reproducing, and who were therefore ill-equipped to correct errors that might have crept into the text. The errata in turn made it even harder to follow what he wrote.

Alas, durable as papyrus has been in arid climates like Egypt, scrolls ultimately did succumb to mechanical stress, moisture, fire, insects and other threats. In the 'economy' of book copying and upkeep, books by popular authors of course received the most investment of time, effort and material. As part of elementary education, foundational authors like Euclid were in steady demand. Authors of only specialist interest, even ones as brilliant as Archimedes, likely rotted on the shelves. Indeed, by the time the Great Library of Alexandria was destroyed, there was very little ancient material of any kind left in it, that having been largely replaced with 'patristic writings, Acts of Councils, and "sacred literature" in general'.[9]

Meanwhile, starting sometime around the first century BCE, a different writing medium gained traction in the Mediterranean world. The codex (from the Latin *caudex*, for 'wooden block') was a stack of papyrus or parchment sheets that were bound together along one edge, like the modern book (though of course originally the text was handwritten). The advantages of this were almost immediately obvious; an epigram by the poet Martial (*c.* 40–103 CE) was among the first to mention them, around 85:

You who are anxious that my books should be with you everywhere, and desire to have them as companions on a long journey, buy a copy of which the parchment leaves are compressed into a small compass. Bestow book-cases [for scrolls] upon large volumes; one hand will hold me. But that you may not be ignorant where I am to be bought, and wander in uncertainty over the whole town, you shall, under my guidance, be sure of obtaining me. Seek Secundus, the freedman of the learned Lucensis, behind the Temple of Peace and the Forum of Pallas.[10]

In addition to their convenient size, Martial extols the sheer amount of text his *membrana tabellis* encompassed: 'The voluminous Livy, of whom my [scroll] bookcase would once scarcely have contained the whole, is now comprised in this small parchment volume.'[11] The economic advantage of a codex edition on papyrus as against its equivalent in scrolls has been estimated at 26 per cent – a not inconsiderable saving.[12] If this sounds reminiscent of a modern flat-dweller praising how much space and money they saved by converting from paper to ebooks, it is no surprise: the movement from the scroll to the codex was the most momentous shift in the technology of publishing before the printing press.[13]

The codex was not only more individually portable, more economical and (with a hard cover) more durable than a scroll. The latter had to be unrolled to find a specific piece of text, much like an old reel-to-reel or cassette tape. A codex, on the other hand, afforded direct access to information simply by flipping the leaves directly to particular passages.[14] This is probably one reason why it became the almost exclusive medium for Christian writings (Bibles, hymnals and so on), which required 'random access' to passages relevant to a sermon, festival or date.[15] Whether it was for this reason or any of the others, the parchment codex gradually replaced the papyrus roll, until the latter almost entirely disappeared by the sixth century CE.

None of this is to say that producing an individual codex was a cheap proposition. Estimates of the number of sheep- or calf-skins necessary to produce the parchment for an average-size codex run into the dozens.[16] According to Diocletian's Price Edict – a schedule of price controls enacted throughout the empire in the early fourth century CE – the price of just one tanned sheep skin was 30 denarii. Hiring a parchment maker to make one quire of four sheets (or sixteen pages when nested and folded) cost 40 denarii. Quality scribes charged 25 denarii for one hundred lines of text. Even if we exclude costs for expenses such as illustrations, binding, ink and quills, the total expense of commissioning an entire two-hundred-page codex begins to sound like a significant investment, running into many hundreds of denarii. For comparison, Diocletian decreed that the average farm labourer receive a maximum of 25 denarii a day.

With these figures in mind, it becomes easy to understand why, over time, the text of many codices was simply scraped off and their blank pages reused. Still, high initial investment meant that not all ancient works were worth copying over from scrolls. Texts by Archimedes, being already rather hard to find, would seem to have faced long odds to make it into codex form.

And yet, almost miraculously, some did. By the fifth century CE the centre of academic gravity in the ancient world had shifted from Athens and Alexandria to the new Roman capital of Constantinople. There, the builder/mathematician Isidorus of Miletus (447–537) oversaw a compilation of Archimedes' extant works, including then-rare ones that were heroically gleaned from libraries all over the empire by Eutocius of Ascalon (*c*. 480–*c*. 520). This collection in turn formed the basis for the codices that under-lay all the Western editions and translations to come, in Latin and every other Western language. (There was also a parallel manu-script tradition in Arabic, rooted at the Bait al-hikmah or 'House of Wisdom' at Baghdad. The Arabic literature includes material not preserved in the Greek, and promises much more, but it remains sadly under-researched to this day.[17])

Modern scholars refer to the three Archimedean *ur*-texts as Codices A, B and C. Thin as this line of transmission seems, forcing the works of one of history's greatest minds into a bottleneck of just three individual books, it gets worse. Codices A and B were lost outright by the sixteenth century, surviving only in copies that can never be checked against their originals. Codex C, the so-called 'Archimedes Palimpsest', was preserved only because it was erased and reused as a prayer book in 1229. And *that* survived because it rested for most of its existence in a remote monastery outside Jerusalem, being returned to Constantinople only in the nineteenth century. It was noticed there by the Danish historian Johan Ludvig Heiberg (1854–1928), who, discerning the faint traces of Archimedes' work under the thirteenth-century script, photographed and transcribed it. Though Heiberg's publication of the Palimpsest did not restore the unmediated voice of Archimedes himself, it was centuries closer to it than anyone had been in nearly a millennium.

Based on how Archimedes builds upon and cites earlier works in his later ones, the order of composition of his existing works must have been something like this:

1. *On the Equilibrium of Planes*
2. *Quadrature of the Parabola*
3. *On the Equilibrium of Planes II*
4. *On the Sphere and Cylinder I, II*
5. *On Spirals*
6. *On Conoids and Spheroids*
7. *On Floating Bodies I, II*
8. *Measurement of a Circle*
9. *The Sand-Reckoner*[18]

Archimedes' reference to his own *Quadrature of the Parabola* in the dedication means the *Method of Mechanical Theorems* must have been written after the former. The oddball *Stomachion* was only provisionally attributed to Archimedes until a partial version turned up in the Palimpsest; it is difficult to place it chronologically in his oeuvre.

Notwithstanding the fact that it appears last on the list, there is an argument for beginning an appreciation of Archimedes' mathematical work with the *Sand-Reckoner*, as we will now explore.

The Day of Brahma

Truth is truth
To the end of reckoning.
Measure for Measure (v.i)

As noted earlier, Archimedes probably didn't scratch his geometric figures in the dirt with a stick. More likely he did his pondering over a tabletop tray of fine sand. Whether this daily activity in any way inspired his most accessible treatise is an unprovable but oddly satisfactory possibility.

Archimedes opens the *Sand-Reckoner* by addressing Hieron's eldest son Gelon, whose honour at court Archimedes obliges by calling him 'King' Gelon. Though in reality, the prince died in 216 BCE, before his father did:

> There are some, King Gelon, who think that the number of the sand is infinite in multitude ... Again there are some who, without regarding it as infinite, yet think that no number has been named which is great enough to exceed its multitude ... But I will try to show you by means of geometrical proofs, which you will be able to follow, that, of the numbers named by me and given in the work which

I sent to Zeuxippus, some exceed not only the number of the mass of sand equal to the earth filled up … but also that of the mass equal in magnitude to the universe.[19]

'How many grains of sand would fill up the universe?' might as well be a Zen koan, meant more to unhinge analytic reason than inspire it. In Archimedes' time, exactly as now, sand grains more or less embodied the concept of fathomless plenitude: 'not though he gave gifts in number as sand and dust; not even so shall Agamemnon any more persuade my soul,' Achilles cries in Book ix of the *Iliad*. The universe, meanwhile, is the *ne plus ultra* of vastness. Simply juxtaposing such concepts, dividing the boundless by the infinitesimal, is not just to flirt with absurdity but to invite it – a fact that Archimedes is not only aware of but depends upon for the power of his premise.

To appreciate how radical this challenge is we need to understand how ancient Greeks ordinarily expressed number. In most literary texts from Archimedes' time Greeks employed an alphabetic scheme that adopted 24 contemporary letters plus three other archaic symbols to represent corresponding quantities:

1 – 9	α, β, γ, δ, ε, ς, ζ, η, ϑ	(6 = ς = Vau)
10 – 90	ι, κ, λ, μ, ν, ξ, ο, π, ϟ	(90 = ϟ = Koppa)
100 – 900	ρ, σ, τ, υ, φ, χ, ψ, ω, ϡ	(900 = ϡ = Sampi)
1000 – 9000	͵α, ͵β, etc.	

13 The ancient Greek alphabetic number system used in most mathematical literature.

For numbers beyond a *myriad* (10,000), the letter M was written with a multiplier above (M^ε = 50,000).

If this seems cumbersome, many historians agree. 'The Greek notation for numbers,' observes one, 'as compared with the excellent Babylonian notation, was really a retrogression.'[20] Lacking a true place-value system or the zero, this system was difficult to learn and ungainly to calculate with. Using up all the Greek letters to represent quantities left none to represent unknowns, which discouraged the development of algebra. Where modern schoolchildren have to memorize only nine abstract symbols, the Greeks' alphabetic system obliged them to learn no fewer than 37 orthographic correspondences between letters and quantities, all of which repeated depending on magnitude. Learning modern multiplication tables is challenge enough for youngsters today; pity ancient Greek schoolboys who had to learn methods to handle all the permutations between 1×1 and the largest commonly expressible number, 'a myriad times a myriad' ($10,000 \times 10,000$ or $100,000,000$).[21] It is perhaps no wonder that among the ancient Egyptians, who similarly lacked place-value and the zero, the verbs *to teach* and *to beat* had the same root. For most everyday calculation, like conducting transactions in the marketplace, Greeks did not even bother with their own formal system but turned instead to a crude 'subitization' scheme, using pebbles and etched lines much like an abacus.

Into this awkward state of affairs sallies Archimedes, breezily promising not only to count a stupefying infinitude, but to *name* it. Like boasting about how he could move the earth with a long-enough lever, this smacks of superhuman confidence, if not outright hubris. Indeed, though Cicero refers to him as 'humble', obeisances to the gods standard for his time are thin in his surviving writings. Much like Pierre-Simon Laplace when asked about God's place in his mathematics, Archimedes seems to have 'no need of that hypothesis'. The numbers alone are enough to guide him.

To fill the universe with sand, he sets out first to posit a size for his 'container'. In this he follows in a tradition of speculation shared with such astronomers as Eudoxus, Aristarchus, Eratosthenes – and his own father, Phidias (in fact, a passage of the *Sand-Reckoner* is where we glean his father's name and occupation).[22] But

Archimedes' purpose is not exactly like those others. Where they were attempting to arrive at real measurements (or, at least, correct proportions), Archimedes is not interested in the actual figures. To show the power of his notational scheme, he is all too happy to overestimate the space he means to fill. So while Eratosthenes estimated the circumference of the earth at less than 300,000 stades (an ancient Greek unit of distance of about 160–92 metres (525–630 ft), depending on where it is defined), Archimedes bids it up to a round 3,000,000. For the diameter of the Sun, he overshoots Aristarchus' estimate and makes it thirty times the diameter of the Moon – obviously too small in light of modern knowledge, but very large by ancient accounting.

The other vital piece of information is how much of the background sky the Sun appears to cover up when seen from Earth, or its angular diameter. Aristarchus' figure was 1/720th of the (360-degree) zodiac, or one-half of one degree. In one of the rare instances where Archimedes reports doing an experiment, he replicates Aristarchus' measurement by sighting the Sun along a measuring rod at dawn, using an adjustable cylinder or disc to find the distance where the latter just covers up the Sun. From that he calculates that the Sun subtends a range of 'less than 1/164th part, and greater than 1/200th part, of a right angle', or (in modern terms) from 0.45 to 0.55 degrees. The latter estimate is a range because Archimedes, in a strikingly astute insight, is aware that he does not read his measuring device from a single point but from a finite area in the eye – or what we now call the retina.

Aristarchus (*c.* 310–230 BCE) is remembered today because he proposed a Sun-centred cosmos almost 2,000 years before Copernicus. To set the table for estimating the size of the universe, Archimedes starts with this model, though not because he endorses heliocentrism. He is more interested in Aristarchus because he posited an extremely large distance between the Earth and the fixed stars:

His hypotheses are ... that the sphere of the fixed stars, situated about the same centre as the Sun, is so great that the circle in which he supposes the earth to revolve bears such a proportion to the distance of the fixed stars as the centre of the sphere bears to its surface.[23]

Now obviously the centre of a sphere is a *point*, which is one-dimensional and so cannot bear a 'proportion' to anything. What Archimedes takes Aristarchus to mean, then, is that the centre of a sphere is infinitesimally small compared to the distance to its surface, and therefore that (by having a similar ratio), Earth's orbit is also very tiny compared to the distance to the fixed stars. (For all practical purposes this is, of course, absolutely correct.) And yet,

I say then that, even if a sphere were made up of the sand, as great as Aristarchus supposes the sphere of the fixed stars to be ... the numbers [named here] ... exceed in multitude the number of the sand which is equal in magnitude to the [starry] sphere.

To give actual magnitudes to Aristarchus' hypothesis, Archimedes adapts a line of reasoning he used to estimate the value of π in his

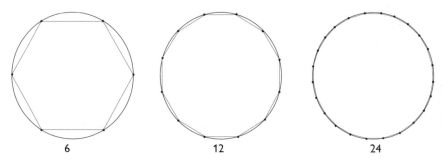

6   12   24

14 Approximating the circumference of a circle by measuring inscribed polygons with progressively increasing numbers of sides.

Measurement of a Circle – namely approximating the circumference of a circle by inscribing a many-sided polygon inside it. The more sides such a polygon has, the closer the sum of its sides comes to approximating the circle's perimeter.

In *Measurement of a Circle*, Archimedes stopped at a polygon with 96 sides, not least because of the difficulty of doing hand calculations with the number system he inherited.[24] But here he has the advantage of an empirical measurement – the angular diameter of the Sun he observed. And so he is free to approximate the perimeter of the 'great circle' of the universe using a polygon of many hundreds of sides. Considering how round a mere 24-sided figure looks, such a prodigiously sided figure would be indistinguishable from an actual circle to the naked eye.

From observation Archimedes knew that the Sun subtends between 0.45 and 0.55 degrees of the circle of the zodiac. Taking the solar diameter as 1/200th of a right angle (or 1/800th of a whole circle), the Sun would therefore fill up one side of an imaginary polygon with 800 sides (an octahectagon). Since he estimates the Sun to be (at most) thirty times the diameter of the Moon, and the Earth to be bigger than the Moon, then it follows that the Sun is less than thirty times the diameter of the Earth. One side of the polygon, therefore, must be less than thirty times Earth's diameter. The latter Archimedes takes to be about 1,000,000 stades (again, an overestimate over Eratosthenes, but one that serves his rhetorical purpose of 'filling' as big a universe as he can justify). One side of the polygon is therefore under 30,000,000 stades wide. As the perimeter of an octahectagon is almost identical to its circumscribing circle, this yields an approximation of the overall perimeter of the Universe:

< 30,000,000 stades/side × 800 sides < 24,000,000,000 stades

Dividing by three, a rough approximation for π, the diameter of the universe is therefore under 8 billion stades. But to make the task of counting the sand that fills the universe seem even more challenging, Archimedes makes it a round 10 billion stades across. (This is a somewhat condensed version of his argument that gets at the gist of his reasoning. The actual text is significantly longer, but is actually one of his most accessible and worth reading.)

This estimate for the diameter of Archimedes' universe works out (assuming 180 metres (590 ft) per stade) to less than 1.8 billion kilometres (1.1 billion mi.), or slightly larger than the actual orbit of Jupiter (average orbital radius = 779,000,000 kilometres). One wonders how Archimedes would have reacted to learn that his effort to project a radical overestimate fell so far short of the truth. Aristarchus, on the other hand, would have reason to believe himself fully vindicated: the stars are indeed very, very far away.

Alert readers would have noticed a bit of a cheat Archimedes commits here: he approximates the perimeter of the 'universe' by measuring one side of the polygon using the solar diameter as a yardstick. But he must have known that the Sun does not lie on the perimeter of the zodiac. Even in his time the distance to the Sun could not have defined the limits of the Universe, since it was known that the planets sometimes disappear behind it. Archimedes remedies this at the end of the *Sand-Reckoner* by making a somewhat nonsensical distinction between the Universe and the distance to the fixed stars, and estimating the amount of sand necessary to fill up the latter. But for his purposes – to describe and use astronomically large numbers – none of that really matters.

So much for the container. As for the counting, obviously some very large numbers are necessary, and extremely large ones were not unknown to certain ancient cultures. The Maya had a name, *alautun*, for a period of time lasting 23,040,000,000 days. Hindu cosmology defines a 'day of Brahma' or kalpa equal to 4.32 billion years. The Buddha expresses the length of the kalpa in terms reminiscent of Archimedes', envisioning 'a huge empty cube at the beginning of a kalpa, approximately 16 miles in each side. Once every 100 years, you insert a tiny mustard seed into the cube. According to the Buddha, the huge cube will be filled even before the kalpa ends.'[25] Unlike Archimedes, the Buddha didn't express himself this way to evoke a specific number, but to give an impression of 'a really long time'.

The Greeks typically had very little use for huge numbers. A myriad, or 10,000, was sufficient for most purposes, such as financial accounting or counting armies. Lacking a place-value notation or the zero, it was obviously very difficult for them to express such multitudes with any precision, analogous to how we use exponents to reduce a number like 4,350,000,000,000 to 4.35×10^{12}. This is obviously a problem if Archimedes is going to reckon all the sand necessary to fill his universe.

His solution is to devise his own system. It starts with a myriad multiplied by itself, that is $10,000^2$ or 100,000,000. The set of numbers in that group Archimedes defines as *first order*. His *second order* is an exponential leap that includes all the numbers between 100,000,000 and 100,000,000 multiplied by itself, or $100,000,000^2$. This is 1×10^{16}, or ten quadrillion – which sounds like a lot, but Archimedes is only warming up. By following the same pattern, using the last number as the base unit of the next set, he can name orders of numbers all the way up to the *myriadth order*, that is, a myriad-myriad raised to the power of itself, or $100,000,000^{100,000,000}$. This is equal to the number 1 followed by 800 million zeroes. If we tried to print this number in ordinary book form, using an ordinary font size and regular margins, the result would take up 1,000 four-hundred page volumes.

From there Archimedes' frame accelerates outwards at truly warp speed. If we define all the numbers in the myriadth order as belonging to the *first period*, then the *second period* goes all the way up $(100,000,000^{100,000,000})^2$ or the number 1 followed by 640 quadrillion zeroes. Following this procedure onward, he finally stops at a number he defines as the 'myriad-myriadth unit of the myriad-myriadth order of the myriad-myriadth period', which is merely $(100{,}000{,}000^{100{,}000{,}000})^{100{,}000{,}000}$ or a one followed by a multitude of zeroes that would make even Brahma blanch. This is equivalent to one followed by 80,000,000,000,000,000 zeroes. For comparison, the number of litres of water in all the earth's oceans is 'only' a bit more than 1 followed by 21 zeroes. The total number of stars in the universe is estimated at 'only' 200 sextillion, or 2 followed by 23 zeroes. The number of cubic centimetres in the volume of the observable universe is 'only' 3.5 followed by 88 zeroes. Even if we had an eternity to write out such a number, we would run out of atoms for ink and paper, given that there are 'only' about 10^{82} atoms of ordinary matter in the Universe.

Again, we need to envision Archimedes conceptualizing such numbers while his neighbours barely encountered magnitudes above 10,000, and struggled with a number system that made even basic calculations cumbersome. Along the way, in order to manipulate his orders and periods, he almost incidentally proves the Law of Exponents – the bedrock principle by which we know that we multiply exponents by adding them (that is, $10^2 \times 10^3 = 10^5$, or $100 \times 1{,}000 = 10{,}000$).

Interestingly, Archimedes doesn't necessarily need to stop where he does. He could certainly name a category superordinate to his *period* (let us call it, say, an *expanse*), and thereby equip himself to count up to the 'myriad-myriadth unit of the myriad-myriadth order of the myriad-myriadth period of the myriad-myriadth expanse'. Likely he stopped because he knew he had more than enough numbers to count what he intended.

So how many grains of sand are needed to fill the universe as Archimedes defines it? Grains of sand on Earth vary in size, but a diameter of 1 millimetre is within that range and works as a nice, round figure. Archimedes, however, assumes a much finer kind of sand, with up to 10,000 grains in the space of a single poppy-seed!

This is an odd choice, more akin to the dimensions of a particle of silt than sand, but assuming such tiny grains serves only to make Archimedes' counting task harder. If we assume that forty poppy-seeds in a line equal one 'finger-breadth' – basically, an inch – then the volume of ~640,000,000 sand grains (~64,000 poppy-seeds × 10,000 grains per seed) would fill a sphere 25 millimetres (1 in.) in diameter. By scaling up this sphere to the volume of a universe 10,000,000,000 stades in diameter, Archimedes arrives at a figure of less than 1,000 units of the seventh order, or one followed by 51 zeroes.

As we recall, this 'universe' extends out only to the radius of a circle he defines by the distance to the Sun. To find how many grains would fill the space out to the fixed stars, he follows Aristarchus by assuming that the distance of Earth's orbit around the Sun is proportional to the distance from the Sun to the stars – that is, if Earth's orbit is 10,000 times its diameter, then the sphere of the fixed stars is 10,000 times that defined by our planet's orbit. This is obviously a much bigger space to fill, but does not tax Archimedes' number system in the slightest. To fill Aristarchus' universe would require 'only' 1×10^{63} sand grains, or 10 million units of the eighth order.

Stupendous as this feat of calculation is, it is worth asking about its larger meaning. The *Sand-Reckoner* was not among the handful of Archimedes' works commonly available by late antiquity. All subsequent versions are descended from Codex A, which was lost sometime in the 1500s.[26] For the time it was available and read, it must have seemed atypical of Archimedes' usual geometrical studies, which often concentrated on deriving straightforward, fundamental properties from seemingly complex questions (for example, a sphere is exactly two-thirds the volume of the cylinder enclosing it).

But the geometer finds no comforting simplicity at the end of the *Sand-Reckoner*. There is nothing in it that Pythagoras or

Plato would recognize as morally edifying science. Instead, the path of Archimedes' reasoning rises in almost hyperbolic fashion into an ether of incomprehensible multitudes, to a place where any frame of reference relevant to human beings is left far behind. To grasp the truth of the universe, he seems to say, we not only must become accustomed to what is almost infinitely large and infinitesimally small, but also adopt such infinities as tools. Indeed, as we shall see, Archimedes' comfort with approaching infinity was one reason why he was a pioneer of what would, thousands of years later, become a fundamental technology for our understanding of how the universe works – calculus.

In this, the *Sand-Reckoner* is most like modern science, demoting humankind from the foreground of creation to a bit-player on a stage unimaginably vast and immeasurably old. At the same time, though, Archimedes shows that there is enormous descriptive power in mathematics. Coming centuries after the Pythagoreans took the fundamentally numerical nature of reality as an article of faith, the *Reckoner* begins to place that belief on an empirical basis. The universe may be far more vast than Pythagoras ever imagined, Archimedes seems to say, but there is *still a number* for all that. It is just not the number anyone expected.

Meanwhile, we recall that the Buddha posed a lower bound for the duration of a 'day of Brahma'. We were asked to imagine 'a huge empty cube . . . approximately 16 miles in each side. Once every one hundred years, you insert a tiny mustard seed into the cube. According to the Buddha, the huge cube will be filled even before the kalpa ends.' If we accept a mustard seed to average 1 millimetre in diameter, then it would take 'only' $3.5 - 10^{24}$ years to fill the cube, or 3.5 septillion. This is trillions of times longer than the estimated age of the universe. But it barely qualifies as a number in Archimedes' fourth order.

Numeromachy

One of the most enduring myths in the history of mathematics attends the encounter with irrational numbers. An irrational number is one that cannot be expressed as the ratio of two whole numbers. The prime number seven, for instance, can be expressed as any number of ratios (14/2, 21/3, 8638/123 and so on), but no such ratio can express the irrational number we know as pi (π). If expanded to decimal form, the value of π forms a sequence of numbers that never ends and never repeats: 3.14159265358979323 84626433832795028841971693993751058209749445923078164062 8620899862803482534211706679 ... and so on, patternless, forever.

According to the myth, the Greeks' first encounter with this unruly class of numbers was not a happy one. Pythagoras of Samos (*c.* 570–495 BCE) founded a philosophic school first in his native Samos, then in Croton in Magna Graecia. Pythagoras is credited for advancing a number of consequential ideas, including transmigration of souls (the idea that one's soul is reborn in another body after death). Perhaps what is most certain about him is that he did not discover the theorem named after him, but was only retrospectively credited for a mathematical insight that far pre-dated him.[27]

The school that Pythagoras established seems, to the modern sensibility, more cultish than philosophical, though Cicero cites him as the first to style himself a 'philosopher'.[28] Members of his 'Semicircle' observed strict rules with regard to dress, diet, sex, exercise – and maths. The masters' teachings were taught but never questioned; to carry a philosophical point, one had only to declare 'HE [Pythagoras] said it'. In this sense Archimedes was a kind of 'anti-Pythagoras': he founded no school, had no disciples as far as we know, told no one else how to live and was keen to hold his own ideas up to scrutiny.

Earlier philosophers such as Thales and Anaximenes argued that certain material substances (water and air, respectively) formed the physical basis of the universe. Pythagoras, by contrast, held that the abstract principle of number represented the cardinal metaphysical reality. As recalled Aristotle,

> Pythagoreans, who were the first to take up mathematics, not only advanced this study, but also having been brought up in it they thought its principles were the principles of all things. Since of these principles numbers are by nature the first, and in numbers they seemed to see many resemblances to the things that exist and come into being – more than in fire and earth and water ... they saw that the modifications and the ratios of the musical scales were expressible in numbers; since, then, all other things seemed in their whole nature to be modelled on numbers, and numbers seemed to be the first things in the whole of nature, they supposed the elements of numbers to be the elements of all things, and the whole heaven to be a musical scale and a number ... [T]he whole arrangement of the heavens, they collected and fitted into their scheme; and if there was a gap anywhere, they readily made additions so as to make their whole theory coherent. For example, as the number 10 is thought to be perfect and to comprise the whole nature of numbers, they say that the bodies which move through the heavens are ten, but as the visible bodies are only nine, to meet this they invent a tenth – the 'counterearth'.[29]

'If you see only nine heavenly bodies, invent a tenth.' That the Pythagoreans did not model their philosophy on the world but modelled the world on their philosophy goes a long way towards explaining what happened next. According to some sources, a certain Hippasus of Metapontum (c. 520–480 BCE) was first to disclose the existence of irrational numbers. Hippasus was a Pythagorean and a gifted geometer who, by constructing the figure of a dodec-ahedron (a twelve-sided polyhedron) inside a sphere, so offended the gods that they drowned him in the sea. At some point this story got conflated with a similar one about the drowning of the 'impi-ous' person who revealed the existence of irrational numbers. This is perhaps because the dodecahedron has pentagonal sides, and the pentagram almost invites the notion of incommensurability (that is, irrationality).

Drowning at sea is a not uncommon fate for those who offend the gods (for example, Icarus, the shipmates of Odysseus and Ajax – the little one – after boasting the gods could not touch him). For the Pythagoreans, the existence of irrational numbers was deeply problematic, undermining their dogma that numbers and ratios of whole numbers underlay the order of the cosmos. Given that the Babylonians and Egyptians had long been estimating the value of irrational square roots (surds), the Pythagoreans likely knew about the existence of irrational numbers before Hippasus. His crime, therefore, lay not in discovering irrationals, but in speak-ing the unspeakable before those 'unworthy to receive it'.[30] The

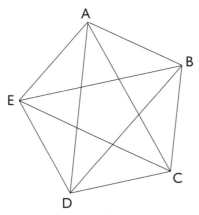

15 A pentagon yields incommensurable sides when side AB is compared to line AC. In this case, AC/AB is the so-called 'golden ratio', or *phi*. The ratio actually appears many times in the pentagram, depending on which inscribed lines are compared.

sources are ambiguous on whether he was deliberately drowned by his fellow cultists, or whether the gods did it for them.

Alas, the demise of Hippasus could not resolve the challenge posed by irrational numbers. As an aspect of enhancing peace of mind, ancient science had an enduring predisposition to 'save the appearances', to find an arrangement that fitted the apparent facts whether or not it was, strictly speaking, accurate. Perhaps the best example of this is the geocentric system of Claudius Ptolemy. His system was based on false premises, based on nothing we recognize as physics, that nevertheless explained how the sky worked pretty well (at least to the naked eye). Since it 'saved the appearances', what reason for mere mortals to challenge it? And it more or less wasn't challenged for well over a thousand years.[31]

If working with numbers led to transcendental monstrosities like π and √2, then perhaps it was the best part of prudence to play numbers down.[32] A geometer can perfectly well work with pentagrams, for instance, without being particularly concerned with the value of the golden ratio, or with circles without knowing π to any particular degree of precision.

A key figure in 'saving the appearances' in Greek geometry was Eudoxus of Knidos (390–337 BCE). An influential astronomer as well as a mathematician, Eudoxus developed a theory of proportionality that emphasized magnitudes, not numbers. While this distinction seems arbitrary at first glance, it is significant because it allowed geometers to observe relationships between properties of figures (lengths, areas, volumes and so on) without concerning themselves overmuch with actual quantities of length, area or volume. And so, when in *Measurement of a Circle* Archimedes opens his argument by asserting that *the area of any circle is equal to a right-handed triangle in which one of the sides is equal to the radius . . . and the other the circumferences of the circle*, it might seem curious that he begins with some other figure to compare the circle with, instead of just getting on with directly measuring a circle. But this comparative approach – relating a hard-to-measure figure to an easily measured one – is what he needs to get as far as he can without resorting to messy, potentially distracting specific numbers.

This emphasis on geometric magnitudes over quantities amounts to a real difference between how we conceptualize maths and how ancient Greeks did. Interestingly, there are still vestiges of this older approach in our language. When we use the term 'three-squared' (3^2), we tend to mentally translate this into its simple equivalent, the dimensionless quantity nine. But to Greeks like Archimedes, 'three-squared' was literally a square with sides of length three, and an area of nine. 'Three-cubed' is literally a cube with sides of three and a volume of 27. For us, the geometry implicit in 'squaring' or 'cubing' a number is something we don't think about. But for the Greeks, the shapes, areas and volumes indicated by these terms were more than figures of speech.

Tales of a 'crisis' triggered by irrational numbers among the Pythagoreans may well be a bit of entertaining mythology invented by later generations of mathematicians. But mythology is not always just fiction. The emphasis on magnitudes over numbers, however it arose, arguably delayed the development of a decimal notation system and algebra among the Greeks. At the same time, it informed a geometry that was, as exemplified by Archimedes, complex, subtle and deeply powerful.[33] At a time when most of the world was content to settle for equating π with three, Archimedes' estimate was the most precise of any known in the world for centuries (with one possible exception). It was definitively surpassed by the Chinese mathematician Liu Hui some five hundred years after Archimedes' death, using a similar but streamlined geometric technique.[34] Interestingly, though Chinese mathematicians knew about irrational numbers fairly early, they did not seem particularly disturbed by them (Liu Hui called them 'little nameless numbers'). This may be because the Chinese had a place-value system for expressing quantity that made complex calculations like extracting square roots much less unwieldy than the Greeks' alphabetic system, and also a more pragmatic, results-oriented mathematics in general. This should serve as a reminder that maths isn't impervious to its cultural context. Though it and the other 'hard' sciences are often idealized as transcending culture because they are quantitative, it is sometimes useful for historians to know not only *what* science was being done, but *whose*.[35]

We have already had occasion to note Archimedes' use in the *Sand-Reckoner* of an inscribed polygon to estimate the circumference of the zodiac. His most famous use of the technique, however, is undoubtedly his estimate and proof of the value of π. To be sure,

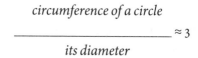

$$\frac{circumference\ of\ a\ circle}{its\ diameter} \approx 3$$

was known for a long time before Archimedes. In the Bible, Solomon's architect Hiram constructed a brass water basin that was 'ten cubits from brim to brim: it was round all about . . . and a line of thirty cubits did encompass it' – in other words, a ratio of exactly three.[36] Evidence surfaced in 1936 that at least one ancient Elamite did much better much earlier, as recorded on a 4,000-year-old cuneiform tablet. Interestingly, this anonymous mathematician did the calculation starting, like Archimedes, with a hexagon inscribed in a circle. Based on the assumption (that is, without proof) that the circumference of a circle is $^{25}/_{24}$ the circumference of the hexagon inscribed in it, they calculated (assuming a hexagon with a perimeter of 3 and a length between opposite vertices of 1) –

$$\left(^{25}/_{24} * 3\right) = \,^{25}/_8 \approx \pi$$

– which is 3.125 in decimal form or within 0.5 per cent of the modern approximation, and obviously much better than the one in the Bible.[37]

Archimedes' effort to define the limits of π are laid out in his *Measurement of a Circle*. What makes this work differ from those earlier efforts, ironically, makes its title wholly a misnomer – it is not about a 'measurement' at all, but a derivation of π based wholly on geometric logic. Today that logic is called the 'method of exhaustion'. Possibly first proposed by the sophist Antiphon of Athens in the fifth century BCE, and formalized by Eudoxus in the fourth, it is a method of estimating the area of a figure (always something non-obvious, like a circle) by inscribing a polygon of known area inside it. The polygon must, by definition, be smaller than the circle because it is inside it. By gradually increasing the number of sides of the polygon, the difference between it and the circle shrinks. The method can yield estimates that are arbitrarily close to the true value, like the estimate of the value of π, depending on how many times we repeat the process (from six-sided polygon to twelve-sided to twenty-four-sided, potentially ad infinitum). A million-sided polygon would, of course, be practically indistinguishable from the circle. Yet in principle there would still be an infinitesimal difference. For this reason, exhaustion can provide only the bound of a *range* that, through sheer repetition (unto exhaustion), we can make as close as we like to (in this case) the true area of the circle.

Archimedes' use of the method differs from Eudoxus' because he is interested in estimating not areas, but the circle's circumference. That will, if divided by the known diameter, allow him to estimate bounds for π. Archimedes not only inscribes a polygon inside the circle, but runs the same procedure on a series of circumscribing (or outside) polygons. In this way he is engaged in double exhaustion, closing in on the irrational number from both sides.

For the inscribed hexagon the pickings are easy: the six-sided figure is made up of six equilateral triangles, and so has sides that are exactly equal to the radius of the circle. The perimeter of the polygon would simply be 6 * r. The real work begins with the twelve-sided polygon, or dodecagon. That figure can be envisioned as twelve conjoined triangles with interior angles of 30°. To find the perimeter of the dodecagon, Archimedes must find the length of the outer sides. To do that, he divides each triangle in half, making two right triangles at the bases. He then uses the Pythagorean Theorem ($a^2 + b^2 = c^2$) to find the outside segments of the triangles ($2 \times S$ in the figure), multiply that by 12 and find the entire perimeter of the dodecagon. (This is, again, condensed and simplified. In the proof, Archimedes utilizes magnitudes (ratios of lengths) and inequalities that do not always make his reasoning obvious – possibly because the work was truncated over many copyings and recopyings. In versions published since the collection of his works in Constantinople, some of the gaps have been filled in by Eutocius.)[38]

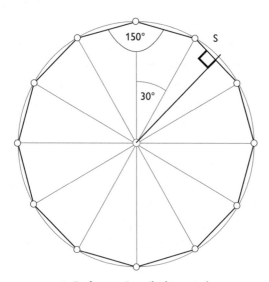

16 Dodecagon inscribed in a circle.

To converge on the circumference, and therefore π, Archimedes laboriously repeats this process for polygons inside and outside the circle, with increasing numbers of sides. Not for nothing was this method identified with exhaustion. In the end, he stops with 96-sided polygons ('enenecontahexagons'). Dividing the results by the diameter, he arrives at an approximation of π of unprecedented precision: it lies between $10/71$ and $3\frac{1}{7}$. In decimal expansion, a form that would have been alien to Archimedes, this is between 3.14085 and 3.14286. This would remain the most precise estimate anywhere for five centuries, and in Europe for a millennium more. (One late source reports that Archimedes' near-contemporary Apollonius of Perga came up with even tighter bounds for the value of π, but Apollonius' work is lost and there is no way to confirm this claim.[39])

It is worth emphasizing that *Measurement of a Circle* is not just an estimate, it is a *proof*. An estimate without proof, like that of our anonymous Elamite geometer, can be the result of many techniques, even physical measurement, and can be more or less accurate purely by accident. As much as the vicissitudes of transmission have allowed, Archimedes has willed us (and I mean that both in terms of effort and of legacy) a range that not only is true, but *must* be true. And indeed, his estimate has stood up since the advent of other methods, from Liu Hui's use of polygonal areas through the modern use of infinite series. These have yielded more precise results with less cumbersome computation. But even modern computer-derived estimates, running now to the hundreds of trillions of digits, are still exactly within the bounds Archimedes placed π, more than 22 centuries ago.[40]

Archimedes expresses his result as a *range*, not a number, because π is a transcendental ratio that can be represented in numerals only approximately. For this reason, the Pythagoreans saw irrationals as a threat to their vision of a cosmos neatly reducible to ratios of whole numbers. By expressing it as a magnitude,

17 Contending with chaos: detail from a *centauromachy*,
Temple of Apollo Epikourios, Bassai.

Archimedes likewise shows awareness that π is a wild thing, contained but never to be captured. In a sense, grappling with π is just another expression of a common theme in Greek myth – the eternal struggle of the forces of order vs the forces of chaos. In the sculptural friezes of many religious structures (for example, the gigantomachy on the Pergamon altar or the centauromachy on the Temple of Apollo Epikourios at Bassai), Greek warriors battle against the antitheses of civilization, whether represented as titans, centaurs, giants or Amazons. In this sense, Archimedes' *Measurement* can be likened to a mathematical frieze, testifying to one very rational man's struggle to contain the irrational.

Curving towards Infinity

Along with his work on circles and irrationals, Archimedes took a deep interest in exploring the properties of the family of curves known as conic sections. These are the curves produced when a solid cone is cut in at various angles. His work was preceded by studies dating from the fourth century BCE, after their use in deriving mean proportionals was realized by Menaechmus of Thrace (380–320 BCE). Finding such proportionals was one pragmatic method for tackling some of the most notorious geometric challenges of the time, such as doubling the volume of a cube.[41]

Today we tend to think of these shapes either abstractly, as when plotted on a system of x–y coordinates, or in terms of motion, as when we imagine the trajectory of a cannonball in the air (a parabola) or the orbit of a planet (ellipse). But that coordinate system so familiar to us (and, depending on the person, so loathed) from our school geometry classes was not pioneered

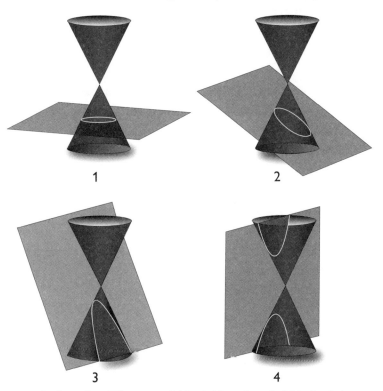

18 Conic sections. When a cone is bisected by a plane, it yields 1) a circle, 2) an ellipse, 3) a parabola and 4) a hyperbola.

until René Descartes, almost 2,000 years after Archimedes died. And the physics of motion was, given the mathematical tools of the time, both difficult for the Greeks to rationalize and doctrinally fraught, given that some philosophers, such as Parmenides (*c.* 500 BCE) and Zeno of Elea (*c.* 490–430 BCE), challenged anyone to prove that physical motion was anything more than an illusion of the senses. (The latter philosopher's famous paradoxes – such as his argument that a runner 'moving' towards a point must cover one-half the distance first, then another one-half of that, and yet another one-half, ad infinitum, and so will never arrive because there's always some next half, some distance left to cover – were meant to demonstrate the fundamental absurdity of the proposition that anything moves.)

For Archimedes, the conic sections were just geometry, with properties that should be as measurable as any square or triangle.[42] But how to measure such irregular shapes? If we imagine a parabola cut by a line as in A, what is the area contained between the line and the curve? One way to approach the problem is to recast it in more manageable terms, such as the familiar shape of a triangle. This is what Archimedes sets out to do in the latter propositions of *Quadrature of the Parabola.*

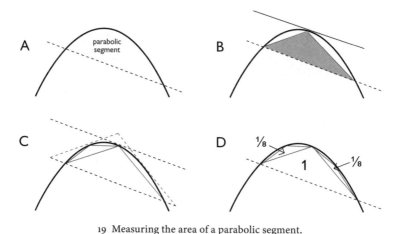

19 Measuring the area of a parabolic segment.

First, he inscribes a triangle inside the parabolic segment, with a base formed on the intersecting line and the triangle's apex on the curve where a parallel, tangential line just touches it (B). The area of the inscribed triangle is, obviously, less than the curved segment. Recall how he measured the perimeter of a circle by increasing the sides of an inscribed polygon, gradually whittling down the difference between it and the circle? Similarly, by repeating the process begun in B, adding smaller and smaller triangles, Archimedes progressively fills in the area of the parabolic segment with a multi-faceted assemblage of progressively smaller triangles (C). Indeed, he can make that assemblage add up to an area as close to the area of the parabola as he likes, simply by adding smaller and smaller triangular facets, ad infinitum.

By clever construction of a series of similar triangles, Archimedes then proves that the two smaller triangles add up to exactly ¼ (⅛ + ⅛) the area of the triangle they are built on (D). And so, by progressively increasing the size of the assemblage by one-quarter of a step, Archimedes can approach the area of the parabola as closely as he wishes.

But what is the actual ratio of the areas between the parabola and the big triangle (B)? Here we encounter the procedure Archimedes outlines in detail in his landmark *Method of Mechanical Theorems*. We will discuss this more below, but suffice it to say for now that Archimedes finds the area by balancing his geometric shapes along an imaginary lever (illus. 20). By drawing proportional relationships between the area of a figure and its 'weight' on imaginary scales, Archimedes leverages his Law of the Lever to, in essence, balance the area he seeks to measure against one he readily can. The answer, he finds, is that the parabola is exactly ⁴⁄₃ the area of the first inscribed triangle.

For Archimedes' contemporaries, this would have have seemed a strikingly unconventional approach to solving a geometrical problem. As we have discussed, Greeks invested early and heavily in

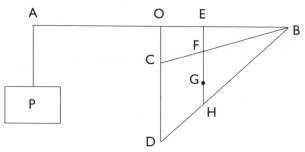

20 An example of Archimedes' imaginary balance. Here he finds the balance is stable with fulcrum at O if the area of triangle OBD equals three times the area of P.

the notion that geometry represented a level of truth fundamental to the ordering of the universe. Like Plato's ideal Forms, the geometry of the material world (that is, actual shapes, areas, volumes and so on) was but an imperfect reflection of the more 'perfect' cosmic geometry that underlay it. This admittedly sounds odd to the layperson, and it is tempting to dismiss it as a particular bugbear of the ancient mind. But many moderns come pretty close to this when they ascribe an almost metaphysical reality to mathematics, whether it is Galileo declaring that the universe is 'written in mathematical language' or Neil deGrasse Tyson tweeting at his fans, 'Math is the language of the universe. So the more equations you know, the more you can converse with the cosmos.'[43] (There is, in fact, no inherent reason why the universe must *entirely* accord with mathematical principles accessible to humans; insofar as our quantitative models always seem to remain tantalizingly incomplete, it arguably doesn't. But these are deeper waters than we are prepared to plumb here.)

Greek mathematicians went further by regarding the fundamental truth of geometry as a system sufficient wholly unto itself. It should be possible, they believed, to work out any geometrical problem solely by analysis, starting from the general (Euclidean axioms, postulates) and proceeding down to the specifics of whatever proof is being sought. By speaking in terms of *magnitudes* instead of *numbers* – numbers, we recall, are inherently suspect owing to incommensurability – no experimental or empirical measurement should be necessary.

And indeed, even though Archimedes sometimes resorted to mechanical analogies, he couldn't accept the method as supplying the final proof. As he wrote to Eratosthenes, 'certain things first became clear to me by a mechanical method, although they had to be demonstrated by geometry afterwards because their investigation . . . did not furnish an actual demonstration.' Instead, leveraging the Law of the Lever amounted to a useful short cut, as 'it is easier, when we have previously acquired . . . some knowledge of the questions, to supply the proof than it is to find it without any previous knowledge.'[44]

And so, by utilizing his imaginary balance, Archimedes provisionally finds that the parabola's area exceeds that of the triangle by ⁴⁄₃. So how did he navigate from a provisional answer to a proven one? Again, he resorted to the strategy of *double negation*: by showing that the area could neither be less than ⁴⁄₃, nor greater, he proves the only possible answer could be ⁴⁄₃. He reasons this by positing that the curve of the parabola is only infinitesimally more than ⁴⁄₃ the area of the triangle, and the assemblage of triangles is likewise infinitely close to the curve (because, as we noted, he can

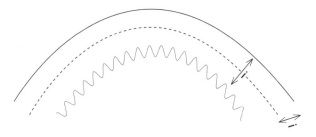

21 The parabola (solid curve) and the ratio of the triangle's area (⁴⁄₃; dotted curve) are infinitesimally close to each other (quantity i). If the parabola and assemblage of little triangles (wavy line) are also infinitesimally close to the solid curve (also i) then the only possible way both conditions can be true is that the curve and ratio are the same.

add as many triangles as he wants to approach any given value). The argument is intricate and resists a short gloss, but the result can be visualized as something like illus. 21.

Method Man

Until the early twentieth century, one of Archimedes' most important treatises, the *Method of Mechanical Theorems*, was known only through a single reference in a tenth-century Byzantine encyclopedia.[45] Three more citations by Heron turned up and were published in 1903, and the work itself was rediscovered in the Palimpsest a few years later.[46]

Obviously, finding a hitherto completely lost book by one of history's greatest scientists is a remarkable event, comparable to recovering a lost painting by an Old Master or a wholly unknown Mozart symphony. But the *Method* isn't 'just another' treatise. It is a key work that, in a real sense, pops open the bonnet of Archimedes' thought process and lets us peek at the engine – a fact Archimedes himself appears to have understood when he sent it to Eratosthenes for safekeeping. If we had our pick of 'lost' treatises to recover, from his vanished works on mirrors and centres of gravity to *On Sphere-Making*, we may well have picked the *Method* anyway (though, truth be told, I'd be sorely tempted by *On Sphere-Making* too). Where the fate of the vast majority of writings from antiquity is largely a catalogue of loss, the survival of this particular book is an extraordinary piece of good luck.

As we have discussed, the *Method* describes a way to investigate geometry by likening lines and figures to weights on an imaginary balance. Magnitudes such as length and area are taken as directly proportional to weight. By observing the conditions under which outwardly dissimilar shapes might balance (say, a triangle balancing a circle, or a parabolic segment balancing a cylinder), Archimedes can readily uncover relationships that he might not have thought to look for otherwise. He could then undertake the laborious process of analysis, his work of 'exhaustion', with confidence that the proof he seeks is there to find.

We have already mentioned his application of this approach in his 'squaring' (area measurement) of the parabola. Perhaps its most significant use was in proving the ratio Archimedes wanted commemorated on his grave: the ratios of the volume and surface area of a sphere to a cylinder enclosing it are both exactly ⅔. Purely geometric proofs of these are laid out in the first *On the Sphere and the Cylinder*, propositions 33 and 34. But now we know from the *Method* that Archimedes knew to look for that proof only because he already had an answer based on an imaginary mechanical experiment.

The argument begins by constructing a deceptively complex-looking figure of a sphere and a cone enclosed by a small cylinder and larger cone, all of which are nested in a larger cylinder. This construct is placed at one end of an imaginary lever. He then

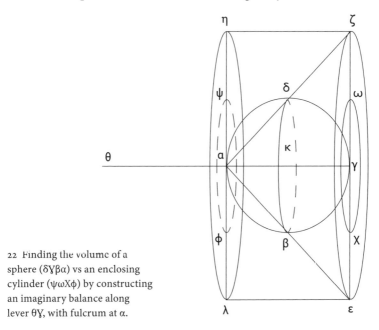

22 Finding the volume of a sphere (δγβα) vs an enclosing cylinder (ψωχφ) by constructing an imaginary balance along lever θγ, with fulcrum at α.

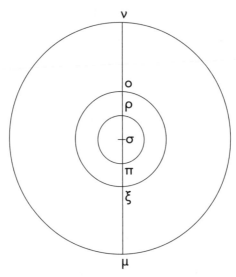

23 Cross-section showing a series of nested circles.

uses a plane to slice through the figure, producing a 'bulls-eye' cross-section (illus. 23).[47]

The big outer circle corresponds to the large cylinder, the next in to the sphere, and the innermost to the small cone. Using a proposition from Euclid, Archimedes deduces that the ratio of the areas

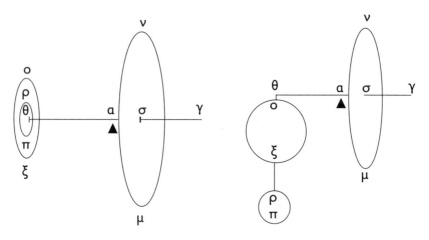

24 Circle νμ balanced in two ways against circles οξ and ρπ, with fulcrum at α.

of the big circle vs the two smaller ones is similar to the ratio of the lengths of his two lever arms, with the fulcrum at *a*.

From his work on the centre of gravity, Archimedes knew that, if he detached the two smaller circles from the big one, it would not affect its position at the latter's centre. Assuming the areas of the circles are proportional to their weights, he can then put the smaller circles at a distance that produces a lever in equilibrium. (Since the smaller circles are together smaller in area than the bigger one, they must be proportionally more distant from the fulcrum.) By the same principle, moreover, he can pop the smallest circle from the larger one on the left side, yielding a Calder-like imaginary mobile that is likewise in perfect balance (illus. 24).

Knowing this, Archimedes also knows the exact proportional relationships between all the circles, including their areas, radii and circumferences. In addition, he knows, based on Euclid, that all circles are proportionate to each other by the squares of their diameters.[48] This enables him to deduce that the volumes of the solids associated with these circles – the cone, the sphere and the large cylinder – are likewise proportional, yielding something like the illustration below. (Note again that, like a proper Pythagorean, Archimedes deals only with magnitudes here, or relative values, not measurements. Nor did he use the algebraic notion below.) The equilibrium, with the objects on the left located twice as far from the fulcrum, indicates that the relationship between the solids is:

Large cylinder / (sphere + large cone) = 2

Knowing this, and furthermore that the large cone is one-third the volume of the large cylinder (Euclid again[49]), he can therefore conclude that the sphere is half the volume of the large cone (for example, if we set the volume of the cylinder at 6, and the cone at one-third of that, or 2, the the volume of the sphere therefore must be 1, or half the large cone (illus. 25)).

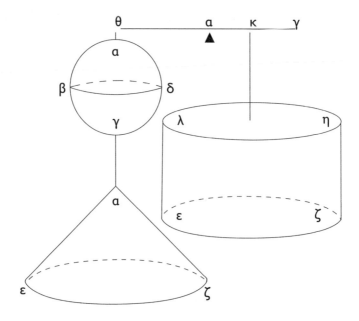

25 Imaginary scale with solids arranged in equilibrium.

We begin to see where this is going if we haven't already: if we know the proportions of the volumes of the cones vs each other and vs the cylinders, and the sphere vs the cones, then we should be able to deduce the relationship between the sphere and the small cylinder enclosing it. In plain English, if the large cone is eight times the volume of the small one, and the sphere is half the volume of the big cone, then,

$$Vol\ (sphere) = 4\ [Vol\ (small\ cone)]$$

Since the enclosing (small) cylinder is six times the volume of the small cone,

$$Vol\ (enclosing\ cylinder) = 6\ [Vol\ (small\ cone)]$$

then the ratio of the sphere to the enclosing cylinder has to be

Volume of sphere / volume of enclosing cylinder = ⁴⁄₆

Or, reducing the fraction, two-thirds.

Thus Archimedes first arrived at the ratio he wanted immortalized on his grave. Or, more accurately, he arrived at the first piece of evidence that led him to prove that ratio by pure analysis, in *Sphere and Cylinder*. This and other propositions in the *Method* are tours de force in deductive reasoning. For those with a taste for it, they almost have the quality of compelling drama, where the exposition is laid at the outset, figural characters are introduced, an argument develops with surprising turns and a conclusion that seemed distant in the beginning feels not only justified but inevitable.

They also offer a telling illustration of how scientific knowledge (broadly speaking, including maths) advances in the untidy arena of practice. In some ways we are all still sub-Pythagorean in how we imagine a distinction between 'abstract' (or 'pure') vs 'applied' science – in other words, between what research scientists do and what's done by the range of practitioners, from engineers to specialized craftspeople to garage putterers. While we are no longer as disdainful of banausic pursuits as ancient elites like Plato and Seneca, we still imagine that, by and large, the vector of discovery proceeds downhill, from the Mount Parnassus of rarified theory down the ravines of 'applied science' to the plains where ordinary mortals live. The upper reaches are populated, we imagine, with titans like Newton, Einstein, Darwin – and Archimedes. The air is clearer up there on the precipice of heaven; we feel Einstein earned the right to demand, 'I want to know God's thoughts.'

One of the most incisive critiques of this top-down view was published in 1962 by the French anthropologist Claude Lévi-Strauss. The title *La Pensée sauvage* is often literally translated as *The Savage Mind*, but Lévi-Strauss isn't talking about 'savagery' in the perjorative sense we have in English, as in 'coarse' or 'brutal'. Nor is he alluding to some kind of idealized ancestor, the Rousseauian 'noble savage'. By *sauvage* Lévi-Strauss means something closer to a 'prior' or 'undomesticated' mind – one that existed from the beginning of modern humans and coexists today alongside the modern logico-scientific one. While we owe much to the latter in how we understand the world now, it was that *sauvage* mind that first tamed fire, fashioned shelter and clothing, smelted metals, made the first art, domesticated plants and animals, and all the other fundamental innovations that characterize our species. It is not 'pre-science' in a simple evolutionary sense. 'This *science of the concrete*', Lévi-Strauss writes, 'was necessarily restricted by its essence to results other than those destined to be achieved by the exact natural sciences but it was *no less scientific and its results no less genuine*. They were secured ten thousand years earlier and still remain the basis of our own civilization.' It still structures many of our ways of thinking about the world today, operating alongside and complementing approaches we think of as strictly scientific.

Lévi-Strauss embodies these complementary approaches in two figures: the scientist, whom he often calls the 'engineer', and the *bricoleur*. The latter is another term that has no easy one-word equivalent in English. It denotes a resourceful figure, adept at adapting whatever materials are at hand to solve a problem, construct a tool or perform any task that demands ingenuity. The bricoleur is a tinkerer, an improviser, an artificer like the Victorian inventor in his parlour-laboratory. This person is goal-oriented, less concerned with the theoretical implications of the means they choose than the scientist. Where the symbol of the latter might be the slide rule or periodic table, the bricoleur's might as well be the butter-knife – a multi-tool endlessly suitable for turning screws, prying open shut things or extracting bread from toasters among a thousand other uses besides spreading butter.

Lévi-Strauss uses language evocative of Archimedes when he describes how the bricoleur might regard their materials:

124

A particular cube of oak could be a wedge to make up for the inadequate length of a plank of pine or it could be a pedestal – which would allow the grain and polish of the old wood to show to advantage. In one case it will serve as an extension, in the other as material.

The scientist, on the other hand, 'questions the universe . . . always trying to make his way out of and go beyond the constraints imposed by a particular state of civilization while the bricoleur by inclination or necessity always remains within them.'

Almost as soon as he makes this distinction, Lévi-Strauss undermines it, noting that 'the scientist never carries on a dialogue with nature pure and simple but rather with a particular relationship . . . definable in terms of his particular period.' Both figures are 'on the lookout for "messages"' from the universe. But the bricoleur is, by and large, most interested in recycling and recasting messages that are known prior, while the scientist 'is always on the lookout for *that other message* which might be wrested from an interlocutor in spite of his reticence'. The bricoleur's 'dialogue' is always pastiche. The scientist opens up a discussion with nature using entirely new terms.[50]

Lévi-Strauss's mid-twentieth-century conceptual framework is foundational for structuralism in particular and cultural anthropology in general, and is of course not the last word in either. (When is there ever a final word in cultural anthropology?) But it is interesting to ask where the ancient scientists, poised as they were between the Age of the Bricoleur and the Age of Science, belong in this scheme. For instance, it has frequently puzzled historians of science that the Greek mathematician Diophantus of Alexandria (*c.* 250 CE) came so close to developing the tools we know today as algebra, including systematic use of symbols (such as using an *x* for a kind of 'unknown') and rules for manipulating them – but left the invention of symbolic reasoning in its modern form to Arab mathematicians centuries later. His best-known work, the *Arithmetica*, presents some 189 unique problems, which he proceeds to solve in ingenious yet entirely ad hoc ways. Instead of developing a general method powerful enough to solve any problem of its type, he addressed only specific examples, tailoring his methods to each. His approach was so unsystematic that one nineteenth-century mathematician noted, with evident frustration, 'it is difficult for the modern scholar to solve the 101st problem even after having studied 100 of Diophantus's solutions.'[51]

In this, we see Diophantus operated very much in the mode of the mathematical bricoleur, solving problems opportunistically instead of erecting frameworks. Though he is sometimes called the 'father of algebra', what Lévi-Strauss would regard as one of the culturally mediated 'tools' at his disposal – the inherently awkward ancient Greek number system – proved too cumbersome for Diophantus to attain that distinction.[52] Instead, our word 'algebra' derived from an Arabic word for 'bone-setting', after the title of a ninth-century CE text by the Persian polymath Muḥammad ibn Mūsā al-Khwārizmī – the man who fulfilled the promise of Diophantus' scattershot treatment (al-Khwārizmī's name also forms the basis for the word 'algorithm'). In this case, at least, it was the Greek who was 'pre-scientific', and the Arabized Persian who put the discipline on a truly systematic footing.[53]

Diophantus wasn't alone. In the *Method*, we see that even Archimedes, historically lauded as the greatest mathematician/scientist of antiquity, was not above resorting to the tools of the bricoleur. For there is nothing inherent about the Law of the Lever that recommends it as a heuristic for solving geometric problems. Instead, Archimedes 'interrogates all the heterogeneous objects of which his treasury [of ideas] is composed'[54] and opts for the conceptual equivalent of a butter-knife – a mode of comparison based on an age-old mechanical device and a metaphor ('let's just think of volumes as weights'). And indeed, there is no testimony from Archimedes himself that he regarded this as anything but normal. It is again a consequence of our own historical position, on the far side of an Enlightenment-era hierarchy between abstract and applied science, that makes it seem surprising.[55]

Little Stones

In our survey of some of Archimedes' mathematical legacy we have several times had occasion to run into the concept of infinity. The method of exhaustion he adopted from Eudoxus, and the stupendous quantities he surveyed in the *Sand-Reckoner* (which, in fact, end only because Archimedes arbitrarily decides they do), flirt with the dangerous notion of what the Greeks called *apeiron*, the 'unbounded'. It was dangerous not only because it invited certain logical paradoxes (for example, Zeno), but because it evoked the terror associated with very profound, very sacred things, not least the primordial chaos from which pre-Socratic philosophers believed the cosmos ('order') emerged, and to which all destroyed things must return. Philolaus of Croton (*c.* 470–*c.* 388 BCE) was a hugely influential post-Pythagorean who developed an entire epistemology based on the emergence of 'the limited' from an unintelligible, cosmic 'unlimited'. Indeed, from surviving fragments of his works cited by others, we know Philolaus rooted his ideas in numbers, including the specific proportions found in musical harmonies.

To be unbounded was not only to be inconceivably large or small, but eternal, at the same time being nothing yet capable of becoming anything, sacred. *Apeiron*, then, carried very different connotations from those its neutral-sounding Latin equivalent, *infinitum*, does for us today. What some historians call the ancients' *horror infiniti* was not just a lazy refusal to face imponderables. It stemmed from the awe of literally staring into the face of creation.[56]

It might be argued, indeed, that today we are a bit too cavalier when we evoke infinity. We often seem to use it as if it is a number; if all the numbers were a deck of cards, we employ infinite like the ace, the ultimate trump card. But infinity (literally, 'without bound') is a concept, not a number. In fact, it represents the very antithesis of our ordinary notion of number, because it is predicated on never being wholly countable.[57] Calling forth infinity literally invites us into a place where semantics, common sense and mathematical logic tie each other in knots – a place where the part is effectively as big as the whole, where some infinities are 'bigger' than others, and where infinity can curl up within finite spaces. The mythological symbol of a snake eating its own tail (the *ouroboros* in Greek) has long been associated with infinity, and possibly inspired our modern symbol for it, ∞. But a better metaphor would be to envision not a snake curled up on itself, but a snake lying as straight as possible, its body shooting like an arrow to the horizon . . . until it meets its own head eating it from the other direction.

Aristotle is keenly aware of the peril of conundrum when he distinguishes between *potential* and *actual* infinity. The geometer who constructs a proof by positing a polygon with as many sides as necessary is using the former, since there is no upper bound on how many sides a polygon potentially may have. 'Hence this infinite is potential, never actual,' writes Aristotle in his *Physics*. 'The number of parts that can be taken always surpasses any assigned number . . . its infinity is not a permanent actuality but consists in a process of coming to be, like time and the number of time.'

But of what use, asks Aristotle, is evoking a polygon with 'infinite sides'? Is that obviously a circle? Definitely not a circle?

Our account does not rob the mathematicians of their science, by disproving the actual existence of the infinite in the direction of increase, in the sense of the untraversable. In point of fact *they do not need the* [actual] *infinite and do not use it.* They postulate only that the finite straight line may be produced as far as they wish ... Hence, for the purposes of proof, it will make no difference to them to have such an infinite instead [emphasis added].[58]

Historically, mathematicians were long content with this distinction between potential and actual infinity. Archimedes largely respects it, evoking magnitudes that are as big or small as he requires for the task at hand. But there are inklings that he was on to something far more consequential in the *Method*, an approach to infinity that much later innovators like Newton and Leibniz used to found what became a key tool for our quantitative understanding of the universe.

Proposition 1 describes how Archimedes used the Law of the Lever to foresee (but not *prove*, in his mind) that the area of a section of a parabola is exactly ⁴⁄₃ the area of a triangle inscribed in it (that is, what he treats analytically in *Quadrature of the Parabola*, see above). As with the sphere and cylinder, Archimedes doesn't just passively consider the figure before him, but actively attacks it, drawing and extending lines in order to construct the basis for fruitful deduction. He envisions something like a parabolic segment/small triangle nested inside a larger triangle (illus. 26). He also draws the line of an imaginary balance, at the other end of which he will reproduce pieces of the figure that are in equilibrium with the one to its right.

He then applies standard geometrical reasoning to prove that the small line on the left side of the fulcrum balances one of the long lines from the outer triangle to the base (as long as the former is proportionally further from the fulcrum). But then, in a stunning stroke of insight, he observes that the same applies to *all the other parallel lines that collectively make up the triangle.* In other words,

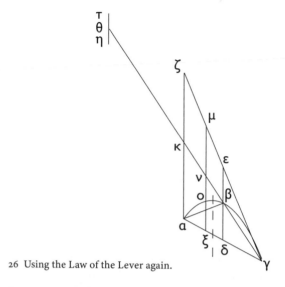

26 Using the Law of the Lever again.

he envisions the triangle as made up of an infinitude of parallel one-dimensional lines, sort of like how a patch of corduroy seems to be made up of parallel ridges in the material. The centre of gravity of that 'system' of lines lies at a place inside the triangle. By balancing the triangle against the parabolic segment (hung from its own centre of gravity, of course), Archimedes shows that the areas of the segment and the small triangle should have a ratio of ⅓.

The details of the argument are interesting but not as important as the larger theme Archimedes introduces. When he almost casually observes 'the triangle . . . is made up of all the parallel lines,'[59] he anticipates how later mathematicians learned to rationalize motion in terms of 'slivers' of time and distance that approach infinity in their smallness and/or number, and, by calculating what magnitude all those slivers add up to (towards their 'limit'), solve problems that were beyond the means of the ancient geometers. The near-parabolic flight of a fired cannonball, for instance, can be plotted in terms of distance vs time, with the distance it covers being the accumulated area of all the infinitesimally thin lines under that curve. The discipline that arose from this approach got a name very similar to what I've been calling 'slivers': today we know it from the Latin word *calculus*, meaning 'little stone'.[60]

Prescient as he was, for Archimedes to have fully anticipated integral calculus by 2,000 years would have required more than just a formidable intellect. Like so many other technologies, calculus required a foundation of other innovations for its development. We have already mentioned the lack of a modern place-holding number system. Without the formalized procedures of algebra, it was far more cumbersome for Archimedes to express how known quantities relate to unknown ones (what modern mathematicians call 'functions'). Without the coordinate system first described by René Descartes (the plots along x–y axes familiar to us from secondary school maths), he lacked the language to visualize those functions readily. The former developed only by the ninth century CE, the latter not until Descartes' publication of his *La Géométrie* in 1637.

Of course, since the *Method* was lost until 1906, it could not have directly influenced the evolution of calculus. True, propositions 6 to 15 of *Quadrature of the Parabola* contain examples of using the Law of the Lever to derive area ratios, and was included in both Greek manuscripts A and B.[61] But Archimedes did not frame that technique in the way he did in the *Method*, as a heuristic essential to his process, and so its significance wasn't appreciated. The key insight, envisioning figures as 'systems' of straight lines, is implicit only, and lies mostly in hindsight. Instead, his anticipation of these momentous concepts remains a curious instance of historical precognition – a conceptual anachronism almost as momentous as the Antikythera Mechanism itself.

Archimedes himself seemed well aware of the limitations facing even the most astute polymath. When he dedicates his *Method* to Eratosthenes, it is because 'I am persuaded that it will be of no little service to mathematics; for I apprehend that some, either of my contemporaries or of my successors will . . . be able to discover other theorems in addition, which have not yet occurred to me.'[62] There is still a bit of Archimedean hubris in those little words, of other theorems *not yet* occurred to him. *Give me enough time*, he seems to hint, *and I would get there*. But even his comfort with infinity wasn't enough to earn him more than his mortal share of time.

Archimedes before Archimedes

Archimedes' achievements as a mathematician, unmatched as they are, did not spring from a vacuum. We have already had occasion to mention such figures as Eudoxos and Menaechmus, who pioneered many of the techniques he refined later. Eudoxus in particular seems to be the antecedent respected the most by Archimedes himself: in a dedication to Dositheus, he equates his own work on the ratios of surface area and volume of a sphere within a cylinder to Eudoxus' discovery that a pyramid is one-third the volume of a superscribed prism with the same base, and a cone one-third that of a cylinder. In as close to an encomium as he gets, he extols the discoveries of 'properties . . . naturally inherent in the figures all along, yet they were in fact unknown to all the many able geometers who lived before Eudoxus.'[63]

Techniques such as measuring the areas of complex figures like circles and spirals by method of exhaustion, doubling the numbers of sides of inscribed polygons to any arbitrary limit, was anticipated by Eudoxus decades before Archimedes. Indeed, historian of science Wilbur R. Knorr has called Archimedes 'the perfect *Eudoxan* geometer' for how thoroughly he mastered his predecessor's methods and extended them (for example, measuring curved figures by 'double convergence', from inside *and* outside, seems to have been an Archimedean innovation). 'The techniques and concerns of Eudoxean geometry run through the entire Archimedean corpus,' writes Knorr. 'And indeed', he continues, they 'define its subject matter at virtually every point.'[64]

Along with his mathematics, Eudoxus was renowned as a philosopher, legislator and astronomer. According to Aristotle, Eudoxus attempted to account for the various movements of celestial bodies by imagining them embedded in a system of nested spheres, each rotating at different rates.[65] This hypothesis must certainly have been known to the astronomer Phidias, Archimedes' father, who in turn must have influenced Archimedes' mathematical education. Insofar as he appears to identify more with the tradition of Eudoxus than of Euclid, we may perceive a trace of how the young Archimedes was first led to mathematics – not just in the disembodied realm of Euclidean theorems, but seated by his father's side, contemplating the complex movements spawned by Eudoxan spheres, in the applied craft of studying the stars.

Even heroes need heroes. If Archimedes' ingenious proofs became an inspiration to generations of mathematicians to come, the example of Eudoxus, mediated at first through the authority of Phidias, may well have served that role for Archimedes.

3

Legacy

As we have seen, Archimedes' works barely survived the long twilight of late antiquity. Unlike the ample remains of Euclid or Aristotle, one set of fingers suffices to count the manuscript sources preserved at Constantinople and in the Arab world. Of the three surviving Greek collections discussed earlier, two disappeared by the sixteenth century, and one was unknown because it was concealed in an obscure prayer book until the twentieth. Virtually nothing from him survived in the Latin-speaking West until one work, *Measurement of the Circle*, was faithfully translated from the Arabic by Gerard of Cremona in 1187. Fragments of *On the Sphere and Cylinder* also appear in another of Gerard's collections, the so-called *Verba filiorum* or 'words of the sons' of renowned Arab mathematician Musa ibn Shakir. What is interesting about the Arabic tradition, observes scholar Marshall Clagett, is that although it lacked a number of Archimedes' key theoretical texts, the Arabs 'nevertheless mastered the techniques that mark Archimedes' work, and in such a way as to show that they had made him their own – in fact they did so much more readily on the whole than did the Latin mathematicians'.[1]

Matters began to change in Europe late in the thirteenth century. Like so many other good things in history, this evolution was an unintended consequence of something very bad: the conquest of the Byzantine Empire by Latin powers in the Fourth Crusade. Though that expedition was ostensibly meant to recover Jerusalem from the Muslims, thanks to the particular enmity between the Byzantines and Venice it was ultimately diverted against Constantinople. The city was conquered in 1204 and sacked so brutally that even the Crusade's papal sponsor, Innocent III, blanched in shame. (The pope excommunicated the expedition's leaders.) In terms of sheer destruction of cultural patrimony, it was one of the worst cataclysms in European history, far worse than what the Turks wrought on the city two and a half centuries later.

Greek rule over Constantinople was restored by 1261, but the city and empire never fully recovered. One consequence of this short period of Latin control was that Dominican friar William of Moerbeke (*c.* 1215–1286) gained access to Greek sources little known in the Latin West. A friend of Thomas Aquinas, he produced influential translations of works by Aristotle and, by 1269, the complete corpus of Archimedes (except for the *Sand-Reckoner*, *Method*, *Stomachion* and *The Cattle Problem*). His was the first near-complete rendering of Archimedes into Latin, and it influenced later translations through the Renaissance.

One avid reader of Moerbeke's edition was a man who considered himself a latter-day Archimedes: Leonardo da Vinci. Indeed, there are unmistakable parallels between Leonardo's lifetime in Italy (1452–1519) and that of Archimedes, including a turbulent political and military context marked by ferocious innovation. In the Hellenistic period, city-states such as Syracuse and Athens faced burgeoning empires like Macedon, Rome and Carthage; in Leonardo's day, city-states like Venice, Genoa and Milan vied for influence (and, in some cases, survival) with aggressive monarchies like France, Spain and the Ottoman Empire. Kings and dukes competed to patronize journeyman geniuses who rented out their artistic talents in exchange for stipends, security and renown.

Leonardo either accepted commissions or worked outright for the Medicis of Florence, Duke Ludovico Sforza of Milan, the Doge of Venice, Pope Leo X and the French king Francis I. Leonardo's own estimation of his talents is on display in a kind of résumé he composed in 1482 for Sforza, promising a truly Archimedean breadth of military invention. He boasts (among other things) that he could offer the duke 'extremely light and strong bridges, adapted to be most easily carried, and with them you may pursue, and at any time flee from the enemy . . . also methods of burning and destroying those of the enemy'; 'many machines most efficient for offense and defense; and vessels which will resist the attack of the largest guns and powder and fumes'; 'covered chariots, safe and unattackable, which, entering among the enemy with their artillery, there is no body of men so great but they would break them' [in other words, tanks]; 'catapults, mangonels, trabocchi, and other machines of marvelous efficacy and not in common use'. He also mentions, as if in afterthought, that he 'can carry out sculpture in marble, bronze, or clay, and also I can do in painting whatever may be done, as well as any other, be he who he may'.[2]

This is obviously an instance where a highly overqualified applicant is tailoring his résumé to the interests of his potential employer. But Leonardo elsewhere betrays a certain envy for the kind of steady patronage enjoyed by Archimedes, as when he wrote near the end of his life:

> Had anyone discovered the range of the power of the cannon in all its varieties and imparted his secret to the Romans, with what speed would they have conquered every country and subdued every army? And what reward would have been deemed sufficient for such a service? Archimedes, although he had wrought great mischief to the Romans at the storming of Syracuse, did not fail to be offered very great rewards by these same Romans.[3]

The almost wistful tone of Leonardo's musing here is matched only by its loose reading of history – there is no record of Marcellus offering Archimedes any kind of reward other than not to be killed. But his meaning is too obvious to qualify even as subtext. He all but asks outright, *If Archimedes was appreciated for his talents, why not I?*

As historian D. L. Simms has noted, Leonardo's mercurial treatment of historical sources led him not only to ask 'what if' Archimedes had invented the cannon, but to assert he actually did invent it. In one of his notebooks Leonardo describes what he calls the *architronito,* a weapon that used the explosive expansion of steam to propel a projectile:

> The Architronito is a machine of fine copper, an invention of Archimedes, and it throws iron balls with great noise and violence. It is used in this manner: the third part of the instrument stands within a great quantity of burning coals and when it has been brought to white heat you turn the screw *d,* which is above the cistern of water *abc,* at the same time that you turn the screw below the cistern and all the water it contains will descend into the white hot part of the barrel. There it will instantly become transformed into so much steam that it will seem astonishing, and especially when one notes with what force and hears the roar that it will produce. This machine has driven a ball weighing one talent six stadia.[4]

That Leonardo was in an antique state of mind when he conceived the *architronito* is attested by his entirely gratuitous use of ancient measures like 'talent' and 'stadia'. Interestingly, unlike the alleged military use of burning mirrors, there is little doubt that the steam cannon could have worked exactly as Leonardo described it.[5] Still, there is no contemporary evidence for the claim that Archimedes invented a steam cannon, let alone one using gunpowder (as Leonardo asserts elsewhere, possibly

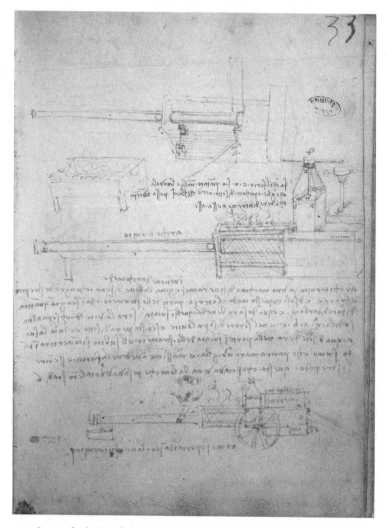

27 Leonardo da Vinci's sketches of the *architronito*, Bibliothèque de l'Institut de France, MS 2173 (Manuscript B), fol. 33r.

following a baseless claim by the Italian engineer Roberto Valturio (1405–1475)).

In line with the prevailing medieval conception of Archimedes, Leonardo's inventions were inspired by the Syracusan's legendary engineering, not so much his geometry or science. By his time, however, the common image of 'Archimedes the Machinist' was already beginning to shift, as a number of Greek texts little known in the West were translated. By the fifteenth century knowledge of Greek literature became a prerequisite for western Europeans aspiring to truly lettered status. Byzantine scholar-refugees fleeing the conquest of Constantinople by the Ottoman Turks in 1453 were happy to facilitate this Greek-inspired Renaissance, bringing their expertise and, in some cases, the texts themselves. As one scholar who had emigrated to Padua exhorted, 'I think the study of Greek literature has been of [such] great use . . . that no one imbued with some study of letters is ignorant of it. For who would be so inexpert and so uncultivated in literal arts as not to know [Greek]?'[6]

Plutarch's work, including the *Parallel Lives*, was one of the earliest and most popular Greek texts to be translated. Selections found their way into Latin as early as the fourteenth century; by 1470 a full translation was published by a German printer based in Rome, Ulrich Han. Plutarch was particularly well received at this time because his biographies not only offered a trove of historical details about great figures of antiquity, but did it in a moralizing context that appealed to the tastes of contemporary readers. It also didn't hurt that Plutarch's Greek was relatively unchallenging, with little style sacrificed in translation.

As we have seen, the portrait of the great scientist in Plutarch's *Life of Marcellus* had a profound effect. In place of the medieval tinkerer, Archimedes suddenly became a preoccupied Platonist, never publishing anything about his engineering, so disinterested in material things that he seldom washed and barely noticed the fall of his home city around him. He became, in essence, the archetype of the absent-minded professor, epitomized to this day by images of a comically unkempt Albert Einstein.

By the time of Galileo Galilei (1564–1642) this Platonized version of Archimedes had already taken deep root. As we have discussed, the story of the golden crown was the subject of Galileo's first treatise, *La bilancetta*, published when he was just 22 years old. At this time Galileo was just a former medical student of the University of Pisa, having left without taking a degree. This apparently did not cost him any confidence, however: *La bilancetta* is a bold work, proposing, solely on the basis of practicality, a revision of a view long rooted in classical tradition. How Vitruvius had described Archimedes' method of calculating the density of a submerged object, by measuring overflow of water, was simply untenable in Galileo's mind, and unworthy of the profound rigour he ascribed to 'that divine man'.

Galileo's yearning to inherit the mantle of Archimedes was an enduring feature of his life's work. In place of received wisdom from such ancient authorities as Aristotle, Galileo held that data derived from experimental observation was essential to understanding God's design:

> These are great matters; yet they do not occasion any surprise. People of this sort think that philosophy is a kind of book like the *Aeneid* or the *Odyssey*, and that the truth is to be sought, not in the universe, not in nature, but (I use their own words) by *comparing texts*! How you would laugh if you heard what things the first philosopher of the faculty at Pisa brought against me in the presence of the Grand Duke, for he tried, now with logical arguments, now with magical adjurations, to tear down and argue the new planets [the satellites of Jupiter] out of heaven.[7]

Galileo's careful studies of the mechanics of motion laid the groundwork for the stately edifice known as classical physics; his observations of pendulums was an essential precursor to modern understandings of periodic systems as disparate as skyscrapers swaying in the wind and subatomic particles changing their states. His refinement of the telescope and discovery of sunspots and the moons of Jupiter were such serious blows against the Ptolemaic model of the cosmos, predominant for more than a thousand years, that they exposed him to charges of heresy. Of his fellow scholars at the University of Padua, a frustrated Galileo implored Johannes Kepler, 'What would you say of the learned here, who, replete with pertinacity of the asp, have steadfastly refused to cast a glance through the telescope? What shall we make of all this? Shall we laugh or shall we cry?'[8]

Besides relying on experiments, however, Galileo emphasized the importance of using the language of mathematics to place his empirical results on a rigorous footing. In this, again, Archimedes is his ideal: in his *Dialogue Concerning the Two Chief World Systems*, Galileo has his character Salviati praise his conversant Simplicio: 'You are an Archimedes, and you have saved me spending more words in explaining to you that, whenever the calculations imply that the two angles A and E exceed two right angles, the observations are to be taken as unquestionably mistaken.'[9] By Galileo's time, when the qualitative physics of Aristotle still loomed large, the rigour and economy of Archimedes' proofs seemed both radical and transgressive. In allowing mechanical experiment to inform his quantitative theories, Galileo was essentially fulfilling Archimedes' vision of a future science expressed twelve centuries earlier, in his dedication of his *Method* to Eratosthenes.

Alas, Galileo himself could not make the transition to the fully algebraic shorthand that now characterizes 'serious' scientific discourse. Having come to mathematics relatively late in his academic career, he was not as naturally adept at it as contemporaries such as Kepler and Christiaan Huygens. For this (arguably unjustified) reason, Galileo's reputation has taken somewhat of a hit lately.[10] But in his admiration for Archimedes he was very much a harbinger of modernity.

The quantitative skills of Isaac Newton (1643–1727) and Gottfried Leibniz (1646–1717) suffered no such limitations. That

Newton was aware of Archimedes' legacy is incontestable: Newton cites the *Sphere and Cylinder* in his 1687 magnum opus, *Mathematical Principles of Natural Philosophy* (or, more simply, the *Principia*).[11] That Newton and Leibniz's independent invention of modern calculus was directly influenced by Archimedes' work with 'integration' of infinitesimal magnitudes is usually dismissed because Archimedes' *Method* was lost until the twentieth century.[12] Indeed, the way Archimedes adds up those infinitely thin 'slivers' of geometric figures by weighing them on an imaginary balance has been portrayed as a way to sidestep direct calculation of their sums.[13]

Archimedes' great translator in the early twentieth century, T. L. Heath, has no such qualms: Archimedes' mechanical method results in 'genuine integrations' in the modern sense of doing modern integral calculus ('it is the *mechanical* solution which gives the equivalent of a genuine integration' [emphasis in original]).[14] But most modern historians of mathematics dispute this for the simple reason that, much like his fellow bricoleur Diophantus, Archimedes applied this *Method* on a purely ad hoc basis. Lacking the notational and procedural tools of modern mathematics, he could scarcely have done more than this.

Newton, for his part, has left a legacy of anecdotes that seem definitely Archimedean. Accounts of neglect of his bodily needs are strikingly similar: it is said that, when he was in the grip of a compulsion to solve a problem, he would become so preoccupied that he would 'forget to eat and, when reminded that he had left his food untouched, would exclaim, "Have I!" before eating a little while still standing. He never bothered to sit down for his meals.'[15] (By the gentlemanly standards of his time, eating standing up would have seemed woefully déclassé.) Newton's version of Archimedes' 'Eureka!' is, of course, the famous tale of conceiving his universal theory of gravity after observing an apple drop from a tree.[16] Like the image of Archimedes running naked through the streets of Syracuse, Newton in his garden has entered our collective lore as an archetype of abrupt scientific revelation.

The Man in the Circle

Knowledge of the location of Archimedes' grave didn't long survive the lifetime of Cicero. There are no further references to it in the literature; beyond the conjectures of eighteenth-century history painters, we know of no visual representations of it from any period. But that does not mean no tangible monuments to him survive from antiquity. There are arguably quite a few. Their connections to Archimedes are just not obvious when we encounter them.

The first example is very far from the Spring of Arethusa. The primary burial ground of the old Egyptian capital of Memphis lies an hour's drive south of Cairo. The Saqqara necropolis, including the famous Step-Pyramid of Djoser, is an essential stop on any tour of the highlights of ancient Egypt. Among the many structures is the Sarapieion, a temple and grave complex originally dedicated to the bull god Apis. Here many generations of live bulls, all exhibiting the prescribed white-on-black markings, were brought as calves, worshipped as living representatives of the god Ptah and buried in state in underground catacombs. Later, the Greek-descended Ptolemies adopted and anthropomorphized Apis into the 'designer' god Serapis, making him the patron deity of their dynasty. It was then, around 300 BCE, that the old sanctuary of Apis was greatly enlarged and adorned with much art, both in the Greek and native styles. (Ptah was, among other things, the patron god of craftsmen, so the investment of so much material splendour on his animal aspect Apis stands to reason.)

Among the surviving works is a curious collection of Greek-style statues known now as the Circle of Philosophers and Poets. Discovered only in 1851, this group of eleven badly eroded figures – sadly reduced now to just seven *in situ* – sits in a semicircle either at or very close to their original positions, though the limestone and mud-brick structures around them have been replaced by a concrete shelter of such surpassing ugliness it suggests a brutalist bus stop.

The shelter is the ensemble's only protection. The statues are otherwise completely exposed to the elements, as well as the hands of tourists and souvenir collectors. To judge from photographs taken since their excavation, the larger-than-life figures have already badly deteriorated in modern times, with inscriptions broken off and pieces of the works themselves crumbling away.

Though they were carved out of a clearly inferior type of limestone – too brittle for the French archaeologist Auguste Mariette to even contemplate removing them to France – the Circle figures nevertheless exhibit considerable artistic interest. Indeed, it has been speculated that the collection represents a second version of another, primary group that once stood in the Library of the Temple of Serapis at Alexandria, likely sculpted out of more durable material. Alas, with even less of Alexandria's Ptolemaic

28 The Circle of Philosophers and Poets, Saqqara, early 1950s.

infrastructure surviving there than in the dry, relatively remote environment of Saqqara, this will likely remain only an intriguing speculation.[17]

The identities of most of the figures in the Circle are unknown and almost certainly lost forever. The name 'PLATO' was carved in the plinth of one, a now-headless man wearing what looks like a heavy woollen cloak, but that inscription has since disintegrated. Another figure holding a cithara, a seven-stringed lyre, bore the name PIND(aros) scrawled on it at some later date. Mariette also reported seeing the name PROTA(goras) on one of the seated figures. Protagoras of Abdera (*c.* 490–420 BCE) was a pre-Socratic philosopher of much influence, making major contributions in the areas of rhetoric, morals and the nature of truth (the relativist implications of his statement 'Man is the measure of all things' are still debated today).

The apparent presence of two philosophers and a poet suggests that the Circle represents some sort of Hall of Fame of great Greek minds. But why they are gathered here, in this dusty Egyptian necropolis? One theory is that the group, collected at a temple the ancient Egyptians thought of as the very doorstep of the afterlife, represents the kind of blessed existence led by worthy souls in the fields of Elysium, spared the torments of Tartarus (reminiscent of the modern quip that 'all the interesting people are in Hell'). Alas, the postures of the eleven figures don't suggest any kind of collegial interaction, no hale and hearty fellowship, at all. Quite the opposite: each seems to be very much an individual, lost in his own individual activities or preoccupations.[18]

Another theory is that the eleven represent the galaxy of great Greek minds who at one time or another travelled to or got their educations in Egypt. According to Diodorus Siculus, it was not uncommon for the presence of these men to be commemorated there:

But now that we have examined these matters, we must enumerate which Greeks, who have won fame for their wisdom and learning, visited Egypt in ancient times, in order to become acquainted with its customs and learning. For the priests of Egypt recount from the records of their sacred books that they were visited in early times by Orpheus, Musaeus, Melampus, and Daedalus, also by the poet Homer and Lycurgus of Sparta, later by Solon of Athens and the philosopher Plato, and that there also came Pythagoras of Samos and the mathematician Eudoxus, as well as Democritus of Abdera and Oenopides of Chios. As evidence for the visits of all these men they point in some cases to their statues and in others to places or buildings which bear their names, and they offer proofs from the branch of learning which each one of these men pursued, arguing that all the things for which they were admired among the Greeks were transferred from Egypt.[19]

It is not difficult to imagine these scenes, with Greek visitors touring such temples and their guides proudly recounting how Daedalus or Plato or Orpheus slept *here* or took lessons *there* from priests in the sacred precincts. This celebration of Egypt's role as mother of Greek genius served the double ideological purpose of both aggrandizing the Ptolemaic kingdom and underlining the deep roots of Greece's association with Egypt (though not, apparently, granting that the Egyptians could be wise enough to rule themselves). Diodorus' list of Greek visitors to Egypt might as well be a list of the eleven in the Saqqara Circle. Was the cithara player actually meant to be Orpheus? I can find no record of Protagoras ever visiting Egypt, but could the name 'PROTA(goras)' be a misreading of 'Pythagoras'?

One figure is of particular relevance to our story. He stands with his left foot on the kind of container used for storing scrolls, left forearm resting on his knee as he leans forward. His right hand holds a long staff that extends to the ground, his grip on it somewhat relaxed, as if he just finished either pointing at or drawing something in the dirt. Although the statue is now headless, it is likely his chin rested in his left hand as he stood, lost in thought over what is postulated at his feet.

There are a number of similar images from antiquity of philosophers and geometers, represented either sketching on the ground or pointing at globes of the heavens.[20] From Diodorus' list we might associate this one with Eudoxus, who lived in the fourth century BCE. But could the figure actually represent Archimedes?

Based largely on stylistic grounds, the Circle appears to date from sometime in the second half of the third century BCE, that is,

29 Drawing of geometer from the Circle of Philosophers and Poets, Saqqara.

either during Archimedes' lifetime or shortly after his death. That he visited Egypt is one of the few well-attested facts about his life. While the importance of Eudoxus is beyond dispute, Archimedes' ancient reputation arguably made him more worthy of standing beside Pythagoras or Democritus.

Though it lacks a head, the dynamism to the figure's posture, the juxtaposition of past activity and present repose, make it quite expressive. It is almost as if the sculptor caught the geometer on the cusp of some deep realization, the gravity of which made him lean a little further forward, relaxing his grip on the staff a bit. As such, it stands out even among other figures in the Circle, some of whose postures seem too generic to qualify as anyone in particular. There is suspended energy here, a suspense that indeed might precede the kind of triumph that drove Archimedes through the streets of Syracuse, telling everyone he saw 'I have found it!'

Alas, the statue is headless, and therefore no help in informing us what Archimedes looked like. Even if the face did survive, and by some miracle the highly friable stone preserved some of its features, we have no other portraits to compare it to, no way to confirm its identity without an inscription. (There is a portrait of Eudoxus in the Museum of Fine Arts in Budapest, of a man in a heavy cloak leaning forward. It bears Eudoxus' name, but it dates to about four hundred years after his death. It is also headless.[21]) That the geometer of Saqqara is Archimedes comes down, alas, to an informed hunch – a hope that some trace of the appearance of one of antiquity's finest minds did survive, somewhere.

The Septasection

To appreciate what may be the greatest of implicit monuments to Archimedes, we have to circle back to his introduction to *On the Sphere and the Cylinder*. In his dedication to Dositheus, he announces that he has worked out several original proofs, culminating with 'any cylinder having its base equal to the greatest circle of those in the sphere, and height equal to the diameter of the sphere... is itself half as large again [that is, ³⁄₂ as large] as the sphere' (see illus. 6). This simple ratio, he asserts, applies not just to the volumes of the respective solids, but to their surface areas as well. The significance of these findings spurs him to indulge in what, by Archimedes' terse standards, verges on a victory lap:

> Now these properties were all along naturally inherent in the figures referred to, but remained unknown to those who were before my time engaged in the study of geometry. Having, however, now discovered that the properties are true of these figures, I cannot feel any hesitation in setting them side by side both with my former investigations and with those of the theorems of Eudoxus on [the pyramid vs prism, and the cone vs cylinder] ... For, though these properties also were naturally inherent in the figures all along, yet they were in fact unknown to all the many able geometers who lived before Eudoxus, and had not been observed by any one. Now, however, it will be open to those who possess the requisite ability to examine these discoveries of mine.[22]

In other words, Archimedes candidly appraises his own discoveries as equal to some of the greatest ever made. Moreover, like Eudoxus, he has uncovered heretofore 'hidden' knowledge: a series of simple relations that were, in a sense, concealed in plain sight, 'naturally inherent' in apparently unrelated figures yet 'unknown' (he makes this point twice). It is this combination of simplicity, universality and obscurity, accessible only to those with 'requisite ability', that seems to fire Archimedes up. While the context is far from what we would call philosophical today, let alone religious, Archimedes' language echoes those of any number of ancient mystery cults (our word 'mystery' derives from the Greek *musterion*, or 'secret'), where initiation into obscure knowledge via certain rituals (for example, the Eleusinian Mysteries, the Theban Kabeiria or the mysteries associated with the cult of Pythagoras) gives the participant access to realms of hidden wisdom, including freedom from death itself. This knowledge was considered so privileged that initiates careless or reckless enough to reveal it to outsiders risked the ultimate penalty.

There is one key difference: unlike the secrets of the mystery cults, Archimedes' 'geometric gnosis' is not meant to be hoarded, but to be shared as widely as possible. The only cost of initiation is possessing the 'requisite [mathematical] ability'. In light of that, and despite his evident pride, Archimedes does not present himself as an authority dispensing wisdom to ignorant minds, not as some kind of Pythagorean *mystagogos*, an initiator into hidden knowledge. Instead, he is merely a scout who has gone ahead and reported new territory.

And yet, this does not mean that the knowledge he shares is any less profound. That a cylinder and an enclosed sphere share a ratio of such simplicity – 2 and 3 being the most basic quantities except for unity itself – is in his mind not just a curiosity, but a glimpse into the hidden architecture of creation itself (compare Plato, 'God is always doing geometry'). Understood this way, it is little wonder that he wanted a sphere and cylinder placed on his grave.

That architecture brings us to perhaps the most visible monument to Archimedes, though (again) his influence is implicit only. In Rome, capital of the state responsible for his death, the Pantheon stands as the best-preserved, and arguably the most profoundly beautiful, building to survive from antiquity. Located on its own piazza in the Campus Martius, its impressive monolithic columns of Egyptian granite and pedimental crown dominate the space before it. But that portico gives no hint of what the visitor encounters within: a vast domed space, 43 metres (142 ft) in diameter, gleaming with original marble, surmounted by a 9-metre (30 ft) hole (*oculus*, Latin for 'eye'). The interior space of the dome is studded with square coffers arranged in five bands, 28 coffers to each band. During the course of the day, sunlight cast through the oculus sweeps around and among the coffers at a just-perceptible rate. Observing the blazing, creeping circle of light, one is reminded of the solar disc Archimedes measures in the *Sand-Reckoner* against the great circle of the zodiac.

Looking from the outside, or even from an elevated position like the Janiculum Hill, that wondrous dome is nowhere near as impressive. This is because the Pantheon, notwithstanding those colossal columns, is not really meant to be appreciated from outside. It is designed to be experienced from within. Perhaps this is why Cassius Dio, who visited not long after the existing building was dedicated, wrote, 'It has this name [Pantheon], perhaps because it received among the images which decorated it the statues of many gods, including Mars and Venus; but my own opinion of the name is that, because of its vaulted roof, it resembles the heavens.'[23] This vault has as magnetic an effect on modern visitors as on the ancients; it is not unusual for tourists to bump into each other as they circulate around the interior, eyes drawn heavenward.

Why such a big structure? Cassius Dio flirts with the obvious when he opines that the building was designed to be a representation of the heavens. Certainly, vision of such cosmic breadth demands a certain scale. The ancients imagined the sphere of the visible stars to enclose the earth like a great shell, which seems to call for a truly spectacular domed space. Someone, exactly who we will discuss below, clearly meant this structure to be an architectural tour de force. After the temple's dedication in 125 CE, the Romans built many other impressive vaulted structures, such as the Basilica of Maxentius on the Forum, but never again a pure dome as large as the Pantheon's. Even today, some nineteen centuries after it was constructed, the Pantheon still boasts the world's largest unreinforced concrete dome. This is astonishing, considering how many architects since, from Florence's Filippo Brunelleschi to Ottoman Istanbul's Mimar Sinan, took it as an inspiration to surpass. The dome Brunelleschi erected over Florence Cathedral in 1436 boasts a somewhat larger dome, but resorts to metal reinforcement.

The empyrean is evoked not only in scale but in detail. The five bands of coffers ascending to the oculus, 28 in each, directly evoke celestial perfection because 28 is one of the 'perfect numbers'. These are the numbers (except 1) which are the sum of their own multiplicative factors. (For instance, 6 is perfect because it is the sum of its factors 1 + 2 + 3: 28 is the sum of 1 + 2 + 4 + 7 + 14.)

There were only a handful of perfect numbers known in antiquity, namely 6, 28, 496 and 8,128. According to the numerologist and mystic Nicomachus of Gerasa (60–120 CE), who published his *Introduction to Arithmetic* shortly before the existing Pantheon was built, these numbers were associated with perfection because of their perceived self-sufficiency, containing all their constituent factors exactly within themselves, no more and no less.[24] But Nicomachus goes much further than this. In his curious work – a book on numbers that contains virtually no maths – he classifies an entire bestiary of quantities, with some numbers having 'too many' multiplicative factors and therefore monstrous-like bodies with too many eyes or limbs, and others 'too few', like amputees or Cyclopses. The perfect numbers are, of course, the aristocrats of numerals, ennobled by their balance. It stands to reason that these would be associated with heavenly phenomena, such as the lunar month containing about 28 days.[25] For if the gods had to pick a number of days for the Moon to revolve around the Earth, would they not be inclined to pick a perfect one? (The Book of Genesis follows in this tradition by having God create the world in six days.) In case anyone missed this numerological evocation in the very structure of the Pantheon, there is also a perfect set of

28 columns and pilasters lining the internal circumference of the building.

The existing Pantheon is the third to carry the name, the first two having burned down in 80 and 110 CE. By that time, either late in the reign of Emperor Trajan or early in that of Hadrian, elite Roman architecture was characterized by the so-called 'ruler and compass' approach to design: exploiting the potential of Roman concrete to be cast in almost limitless forms, architects like Apollodorus of Damascus (d. *c.* 130 CE) applied geometrical principles to create curvilinear designs of such intricacy that they were not rivalled in the West until the Renaissance. As described by Vitruvius, the process began with a basic unit, such as a circle of set diameter, that was replicated or transposed to create almost baroquely complex figures that, because of their modular design, nevertheless retained an overall harmony. These tools were, of course, basic equipment for doing geometry, as Archimedes did at his tray of sand. To be an architect in this period therefore demanded that one be a geometer as well, with any competent designer expected to be comfortable with the intricacies of Euclidean geometry.[26]

For a temple intended to model the majesty of the cosmos, it stands to reason to invoke the greatest geometer of all. For the third and final incarnation of the Pantheon, the architects (possibly Apollodorus himself) appropriated a version of what Archimedes placed on his tomb: a sphere enclosed by a cylinder. If we imagine the inner surface of the vault to describe half of a sphere, then the full sphere extends exactly to the building's ground level, 150 Roman feet below. The cylinder is defined by the external, drum-like surface of the building.

The overall design looks like what Derek de Solla Price envisioned for Archimedes' tomb, if the sphere and cylinder were represented sculpturally – an enclosed sphere rendered visible because the upper part of the cylinder is cut away. This cutaway

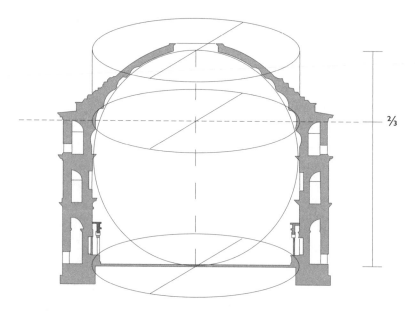

30 The imaginary sphere defined by the inner surface of the Pantheon's dome, enclosed by the cylinder corresponding to the drum.

scheme is why the dome looks far more impressive from the inside than the outside. The interior hemisphere of the vault actually springs from halfway up the drum. Viewed from outside, reinforcing bands – designed to help keep the weight of the enormous dome from splitting the drum – ascend another 14 metres (46 ft), reducing the apparent volume of the enclosed sphere to something like one-quarter of its total.

Apollodorus was one of a select few ancient Roman architects we know by name. Born in Syria, he first came into contact with Emperor Trajan in Damascus, where he was subsequently invited to perform engineering services for the emperor's wars against Dacia. His designs for the Roman army, including ingenious beaked 'tortoises' for sieges, hoists for raising observers above walls, mechanisms for drilling into and breaking masonry and floating bridges, make his military innovations almost Archimedean in breadth and spirit, although some of these may be later inventions inserted into the text of his only surviving treatise, the *Poliorketika* (On Siegecraft).

Though attribution of specific buildings to individual architects is a dicey proposition for a time when all credit went to the sponsor, it is generally accepted that Apollodorus went on to design a number of important structures, including the Basilica Ulpia, Trajan's Baths, a massive bridge across the Danube, Trajan's Column and very possibly the Pantheon. According to Cassius Dio, he met his end under Trajan's successor Hadrian, who was not only an architectural dilettante but highly sensitive:

> Hadrian ... banished and later put to death Apollodorus, the architect, who had built the various creations of Trajan in Rome – the forum, the odeum and the gymnasium. The reason assigned was that he had been guilty of some misdemeanour; but the true reason was that once when Trajan was consulting him on some point about the buildings he had said to Hadrian, who had interrupted with some remark: 'Be off, and draw your gourds. You don't understand any of these matters.'[27]

By 'Go draw your gourds', or perhaps 'Go play with your pumpkins', Dio is referring to Hadrian's fondness for the kind of pumpkin-like segmented vaults that can still be seen in surviving fragments of his villa in Tivoli, such as the 'Serapeum'. Some modern historians cast doubt on this anecdote because it smacks of the kind of scurrilous rumour that always circulates around royal courts. But Apollodorus was clearly on thin ice after his patron, Trajan, died in 117. The architect may well have served blunt objections when the roadway of his Danube bridge, a true wonder of the ancient world, was dismantled on Hadrian's orders, ostensibly for security reasons. When Hadrian came to him with his amateur design for the Temple of Venus and Rome, the architect, by this time probably in his sixties or seventies, did not mince words, observing that the seated statues designed for the sanctuary were too big to stand up in their own temple. This candour (more akin to a wisecrack, as statues too big to stand or pass through the doors of their temples weren't particularly unusual) apparently represented strike three against Apollodorus, and he was invited to leave Rome for good.

Almost unanimous tradition also credits Apollodorus with designing Trajan's Column, which survives close to the Forum he also designed.[28] This spectacularly innovative monument represents Trajan's Dacian wars in the form of a continuous relief that spirals almost 30 metres (100 ft) to the summit, where a statue of the emperor was placed. (Apollodorus himself is said to be represented in the relief, standing before his ill-fated bridge.) One particularly Archimedean feature of the Column is the spiral staircase embedded inside the drums that compose it. The structure is essentially a spiral enclosed in a tube, much like the water-lifting screw conventionally ascribed to Archimedes.

The Pantheon's designer may have meant to evoke Archimedean geometry in yet another way. When modern visitors gaze up at the interior surface of the dome, they don't necessarily find the near-perfect regularity of the coffers (again, five latitudinal bands of 28) the most impressive aspect of the building. In this age of mechanically assisted design, the precision demanded by this is all too easy to overlook. Yet if even one of the bands was slightly 'off', the error would compound throughout the design, resulting in obvious flaws. That it looks as perfect as it does is perhaps even more miraculous considering that the surface of the dome is not absolutely hemispherical, and has become less so over the centuries as the building has aged.[29]

But dividing up a circle into 28 equal parts – or, equivalently, a right angle into seven – was actually a variation on one of the handful of enduring problems in ancient geometry, the 'trisection of a given angle'. Dividing an angle into an even number of equal parts (like two) is trivially easy and has been known for millennia. But dividing one precisely in three (or in any odd number of parts, using only compass and straight-edge) is not so obvious. Indeed, it was suspected to be impossible long before Karl Frederick Gauss formally proved it couldn't be done, 2,000 years after Archimedes' death.

The first practical advance in finding a workaround method didn't come until the fifth or fourth centuries BCE, when a supplemental tool was suggested, perhaps by Hippias of Elis (d. *c.* 400 BCE). The so-called 'quadratrix' was the curve produced by the intersection of two lines – one descending along the horizontal, the other sweeping like the hands of a clock from the angle's origin, at equal and uniform speeds relative to each other. In the left figure below (illus. 31) we imagine horizontal line starting at A moving downwards at a steady rate towards the X axis, while the line from origin D sweeps downwards like a clock hand at the same rate. The intersections yield curve AX. We then divide the Y axis into any number of equal parts (here, seven) and extend horizontal lines to intersect the curve. The lines from the origin to the intersections (for example, DY) define equal subdivisions of the right angle. The useful consequence of this is to produce a curve where the length

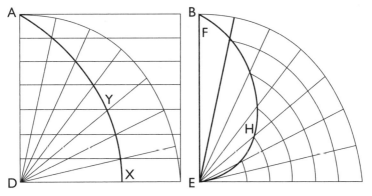

31 Hippias' quadratrix (*left*) vs Archimedes' spiral (*right*).

of a line segment on the Y axis is directly proportional to the angle swept by the clock-hand line. And since dividing straight lines is easy, Hippias' handy 'prop' allows a proportional angle of any fraction (including thirds or sevenths) to be simply read from the lines' points of intersection.

There is some evidence that Archimedes was also interested in dividing angles into odd numbers of parts, such as in the construction of regular heptagons (seven-sided figures). For reasons closely related to trisection problems, the heptagon happens to be the polygon with the least number of sides that is impossible to construct using compass and straight-edge. A scholar working at the House of Wisdom in Abbascid Baghdad, Thabit ibn Qurra al Harrani (c. 836–901), claimed that Archimedes was the author of a treatise on division of a circle into seven equal parts. Thabit's Arabic translation of the mutilated Greek text, much recopied over the centuries and appearing in German only in 1927, is not generally included among the canonical works of Archimedes, and may only be a case of later geometers ascribing it retrospectively to him.[30] But the challenge of constructing such an 'impossible' figure seems like just the kind of problem to spark Archimedes' competitive instincts.

A somewhat more elegant solution to the problem of trisecting the angle than Hippias' quadratrix can be derived from Archimedes' *On Spirals*. Proposition 14 describes a kind of spiral produced when a point moves steadily outward along a line that is simultaneously rotating at a steady rate around the origin (imagine the path traced by an ant crawling outward along the moving second hand of a clock). This produces, in essence, a path where the distance from the origin is proportional to the angle swept out by the clock hand. In the rightmost figure shown previously (illus. 31), a point on a line emanating from the origin that is sweeping counterclockwise at a steady rate will yield the curve EF. The length of a line from origin E to any given point on the curve is exactly proportional to its angle from the X axis. If we divide the length of the curve into (for instance) sevenths and connect the dividing points to the origin (for example, EH) we can therefore equally subdivide the right angle into seven equal parts.

Like the quadratrix, the so-called 'Archimedes spiral' sets up consistent relationships between straight lines (in this case, the straight-line distance from the origin to any point on the spiral) and any given angle. An angle's trisection or division into seven (its 'septasection'?) would therefore be a matter of dividing the radius into however many parts are sought and connecting the corresponding intersections.

Is this how the dome of the Pantheon was divided into 28 parts? While the geometry is sound, how to actualize the method in plaster and cement is not so apparent, and is in fact a matter of much debate.[31] However it was done, the precision in the surviving structure is astonishing, with the angles of the meridians differing from the ideal ($360/28 = 12.85°$ or $12° 51'$) by mere tenths of individual degrees.[32] Though this exactness doesn't get as much attention as the sheer physical magnitude of the dome, the union of these disparate qualities, of precision seamlessly scaled up, is

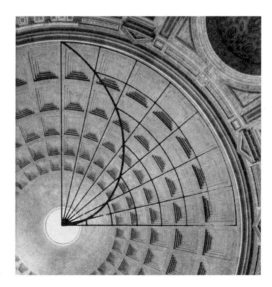

32 'Archimedes spiral' superimposed on the dome of the Pantheon.

another reason the Pantheon is one of the most sublime buildings ever constructed.

The septasection has an additional connection to our probable architect, Apollodorus. The Column of Trajan is constructed out of 29 blocks, nineteen of which have sections of spiral staircase hewn inside of them. When stacked on top of each other, these sections create a continuous stairway that allows access to the top of the monument. Each 360-degree turning of this staircase is completed in fourteen steps, which is essentially the same problem as dividing a circle into 28. Why was this scheme chosen, and not some easier one, some more straightforward division of the circle into, say, twelve or eighteen steps?

Whatever the rationale, it seems to suggest either a taste for Archimedean showboating or a perverse preoccupation with doing things the hard way. The interior staircase of the Column, after all, would hardly have been as publicly visible as, say, the coffers of the Pantheon dome. Who else but a few sophisticated individuals – those initiated in geometric *gnosis* – would even have been aware of the extra effort necessary to plan this division? (Perhaps no respectable numerologist wanted to encounter a 'monstrous' number like twelve in the darkened depths of the Column . . .)

Whether it was Hippias' or Archimedes' methods that informed his work, a direct line can be drawn between Apollodorus' status as an immigrant from the Greek-speaking eastern half of the empire, and the intellectual underpinnings of his geometricizing architecture. This was the culmination of a long process of synthesis of Greek abstraction and Roman practical ingenuity. Generations earlier, Cicero lamented, 'Among those Greeks, geometry was held in the highest esteem, and therefore nothing was more illustrious than mathematics; but we have limited this art to measuring and reasoning.'[33] The Pantheon represents the ultimate bridging of this divide. Roman inventiveness gave its builders the means to erect a monument that was, in certain ways, never surpassed. But it was the mathematical tradition that culminated with Archimedes that gave their conquerors something truly worth building.

Late antiquity boasted one worthy successor to Apollodorus' Pantheon. After the empire's capital was relocated to Byzantium (renamed Constantinople) in the fourth century, the trappings of Roman power were replicated there. By the sixth century one of the Eastern Empire's most vigorous emperors, Justinian (482–565), conceived of building a church that would surpass all others.

Hagia Sophia (Church of Holy Wisdom) was consecrated in 537. The design by architects Anthemius of Tralles and Isidore of Miletus evokes the Pantheon even as it inspired a lineage of great successors. Its most notable feature, the great dome, is wondrously described by the historian Procopius (b. *c.* 500): 'A spherical-shaped dome standing upon this circle makes it exceedingly beautiful: from the lightness of the building, it does not appear to rest upon a solid foundation, but to cover the place beneath as though it were suspended from heaven by the fabled golden chain.'[34]

Procopius' contemporary Paul the Silentiary (520–580) offers breathless prose poems describing the overall effect of the building on onlookers:

> Above all rises into the immeasurable air the great helmet [of the Dome], which, bending over, like the radiant heavens, embraces the church ... Everywhere the walls glitter with wondrous designs ... A thousand [lamps] within the temple show their gleaming light, hanging aloft by chains of many windings. Some are placed in the aisles, others in the centre or to east and west, or on the crowning walls, shedding the brightness of flame. Thus the night seems to flout the light of day and be itself as rosy as the dawn ...[35]

In its prime, long before its reduced state today, Hagia Sophia arguably surpassed any ancient building in how light animated its interior. Along with the flickering lamps, and the columns of light admitted through the dome, the jewels and stupendous abundance of marble and gold and silver gilding, the church had the effect (in Paul the Silentiary's words) of 'expelling clouds of care and filling the mind with joy'. The Pantheon, by comparison, depended for illumination on light admitted from outside, and mostly from the great circle of sunlight projected through the oculus. The differing virtues of these two approaches – one stirring reverent awe in a form outwardly clean and severe, the other embracing a spirit of complexity and resplendence – more or less encompass the contrasting aesthetics of Augustan and Justinianic art in general.

Though the church attempts to rival the celestial dome of the Pantheon, Anthemius and Isidore's tribute couldn't quite match the latter in sheer size. Hagia Sophia's dome is significantly smaller, 'only' about two-thirds the diameter, and is also set 10 metres higher. It therefore doesn't replicate the Archimedean 'sphere in a cylinder' design of the Pantheon, where the diameter of the projected sphere exactly matches the height and breath of the drum enclosing it.

Floating Body

And yet, there is no doubt that the two primary architects of Hagia Sophia were keenly aware of the legacy of Archimedes, almost eight centuries after the latter's death. Anthemius (c. 474–534) hailed from a family that included noted physicians, a jurist and a grammarian. (Indeed, Anthemius may have shared with Archimedes a similarly bookish but non-ennobled background.) His range of expertise was impressive and had a definite Archimedean ring: according to the historian Agathias (536–582), at the vital garrison town of Daras, on the border with the Sassanid Persian Empire, Anthemius was responsible for damming the river Cordes and diverting it through a subterranean channel. With this, he simultaneously ensured the town's water supply during sieges and withheld river access to enemies. He also made original contributions to the mathematics of conic sections, described how to construct an ellipse using string and pins, and wrote an influential treatise on burning mirrors. It stands to reason that Justinian would look to a man of such varied talents to build what was intended to be the greatest temple – not just the greatest church – ever constructed.

Agathias also records a few other telling anecdotes about Anthemius. He apparently lived in a house that shared a party wall with one owned by a certain Zenon, a courtier with a particular reputation for eloquence. A dispute arose between the neighbours, possibly over the construction of a balcony that spoiled Anthemius' view. The neighbours went to court, but as Anthemius had no answer to Zenon's rhetorical skills, he lost. The engineer got his revenge by building a contraption reminiscent of Leonardo's *archichronito*, using bronze kettles fitted with leather tubes. By boiling water in the kettles, Anthemius built up a head of steam that he could release explosively against the floor of Zenon's apartment. 'Striking continuously against the roof it shook the entire room above and overturned its furniture,' writes Agathias:

> And those staying with Zenon awakened and were afraid and went out into the street, screaming and amazed at the marvel. Zenon, wandering in the public places, inquired of his friends how the earthquake had seemed to them, and why they were not killed. And they replied 'shut up' and 'go away' and 'it never happened'.[36]

Zenon apparently caught on to Anthemius' tricks when the engineer contrived a 'thunderstorm' in his rooms using a concave mirror for 'lightning' and noisemakers for 'thunder'. But even Zenon's best rhetorical tropes ('How can I contend against Zeus the Thunderer ...?') compelled Justinian to punish his resourceful engineer.

Alas, Anthemius died three years before the great church was complete. The final phases of construction were overseen by his colleague Isidorus of Miletus, whom we have already encountered in connection with the collection of and commentary on Archimedes' works by Eutocius. Multiple references there to 'Isidorus our great teacher' suggest that Isidorus ran a school for engineers and architects. The collection of Archimedes' works may well have been undertaken to provide textbooks for students of his academy. One possible alumnus was his nephew, also named Isidorus (*c.* 510–563). When his uncle's original dome partially collapsed in an earthquake in 557, it was the younger Isidorus who designed and executed repairs. Elements of his work stand today in the building, almost fifteen centuries later.

Overall then, while Archimedes' name appears nowhere on any of these monuments, his influence remains always under the surface and occasionally still bobs into view. Apollodorus, Anthemius and Isidorus were all leading *mechanopoioi* of their times, and all of them measured their careers against his legacy – as did Leonardo and Galileo many centuries later. Like knowledge of the simple ratios hiding in deceptively complex figures, knowledge of Archimedes became a kind of privilege for a small circle of informed minds, tending the flame of a humble cult for a man who never wanted a cult at all.

You Too, Who Must Be Remembered

You too, who must be remembered,
Won the tears of the general
You defender of the fatherland
Such great ruin striking you
While you were undisturbed in mind
and concentrating on your figures in the dust.[37]

Silius Italicus (*c.* 25–103 CE) does something unique in his epic poem on the Second Punic War: across a gulf of three centuries, he addresses Archimedes directly. It may be this very distance that lent Silius the licence to treat the great geometer in such familiar terms. While Archimedes was almost universally admired in antiquity, his was not the sort of reputation that necessarily elicited great warmth. Yet in Silius' account of his death, there is such pathos in the equanimity of his last moments that it won the tears of a general.

It bears noting that the traditional Roman virtue of *gravitas* seldom afforded opportunity for such displays. Aside from a weeping Marcellus at the gates of Syracuse, we hear that Caesar wept before a statue of Alexander the Great, and the younger Scipio Africanus loosed tears as Carthage burned. In both cases, the sadness seems to stem from recognition of similarity, of a realization that between conqueror and conquered lies not much more than the caprice of Fate. Archimedes therefore joins the greatest empire-builder before Rome and Rome's greatest geopolitical rival as worthy of a general's tears. Indeed, Silius works explicitly to find a kind of similarity between Archimedes and Marcellus, the former a 'defender of the fatherland' and the latter 'in saving the city [re]founded it', all but explicitly making it seem as if they served on the same side. Archimedes' ingenuity enshrined in legend Marcellus' struggle to overcome it. Marcellus' tears are the ultimate tribute a victor can bestow on the nobly vanquished. By spurring his readers to remember both, Silius forever joins them together in renown.[38]

Tiberius Catius Asconius Silius Italicus was an orator and senator before he devoted himself to poetry. His rhetorical skills shone most in the courtroom, where he regularly secured convictions of persons targeted by his patron, Emperor Nero (r. 54–68 CE). Overall he seems to have been more a gifted courtier than a politician, being effective yet inoffensive enough to prosper over a long career. He retired to his estates while still relatively young, barely over fifty, and devoted himself entirely to artistic pursuits. Though his *Punica* is the longest Latin poem to survive from antiquity, it was rediscovered only in 1417, and its modern influence has been slight. But there are signs that Silius' stock may be set to rise.

One further detail suggests there was more to him than truckling under despots like Nero. 'Silius,' writes Martial, 'who possesses the lands that once belonged to the eloquent Cicero, celebrates funeral obsequies at the tomb of the great Virgil. There is no one that either Virgil or Cicero would have preferred for his heir, or as guardian of his tomb and lands.'[39] Indeed, Silius found the tomb of Virgil tended by just one destitute caretaker: 'There remained but one man, and he a poor one, to honour the nearly deserted ashes, and revered name, of Virgil. Silius determined to succour the cherished shade; Silius, a poet, not inferior to Virgil himself, consecrated the glory of the bard.'[40]

While we can put aside Martial's overly generous assessment of Silius' talent, his care of Cicero's old estate (possibly at Tusculum) and the tomb of Virgil resonates with significance regarding Archimedes, 'he who must be remembered'. Cicero, like any good Roman, tends to the tomb of his antecedents, among whom he proudly includes Archimedes. When Cicero dies, it is the turn of his descendants to take over that task. In his respect for Rome's greatest orator and greatest epic poet, Silius adds himself to a lineage that, by association, includes antiquity's greatest scientist.

Given that Silius made extensive use of the histories of Livy and Polybius, there can be no doubt he was well aware of the legacy of Archimedes, and aware too of the irony that it came to be the turn of Cicero – similarly revered in death, but vanquished by anti-republican forces as utterly as Syracuse – to be saved from physical oblivion. The tomb of Archimedes itself was likely long forgotten by Silius' time, but the estate of its rediscover, Cicero, was still there to be preserved. Indeed, there may have been a hint of republican sympathy (or at least of nostalgia) implicit in Silius' rescue of

Cicero's property – an odd gesture for a man who made a career of being an imperial informer and attack dog. Politics then, as now, made for strange bedfellows.

A Body at Rest

Like the snake of infinity devouring its tail, we return to where we began: the lost grave of Archimedes. As we have seen, Cicero is our sole surviving eyewitness to its location and appearance. According to our man from Arpinum, the tomb lay not far outside Syracuse's Achradina Gate, in a necropolis that was already neglected in the first century BCE. While the gate should serve as a telling topographic clue, the centuries have not been kind to the walls – let alone their openings – that defined the four quarters of the ancient city, including Ortygia ('Nasos'), Tyche, Neapolis and Achradina.[41] Reconstructing their locations has been an ongoing challenge for archaeologists attempting to connect the topography of the city with the momentous events that occurred in it.

That is not to say there has been a shortage of attempts. One was published in London in 1851 by John Murray for an edition of George Grote's *History of Greece*. This map includes a 'necropolis' nestled just to the south of the Archadina circuit, corresponding broadly to the area around the modern train station. Unlike the surviving Dionysian Walls that ring the plateau of Epipolae, however, there is not much archaeological support for the positions of the other fortifications in Murray's map. Instead, they seem to be based on the *hmm-they-ought-to-lie-right-about-here* school of historical surveying.

Excavations have revealed that a large burial ground existed in the vicinity, starting from the very foundation of the city. Based on foundational work by archaeologist Paolo Orsi in the late nineteenth century, we know that the so-called Fusco necropolis expanded over time in a generally western direction, with graves from the fifth century BCE to the west of the modern railway station, and ones from Archimedes' time in the Tor di Conte and Contrada Canalicchio regions. Many of the older tombs were destroyed late in the fourth century and early in the third century BCE residential districts spread over them.[42]

What does this mean for locating Archimedes' final resting place? If we follow Tzetzes and accept that he was buried in the 'tombs of his fathers', then Archimedes would likely not have ended up in the later, Hellenistic-era extensions of the necropolis, but instead in the much older section. This would accord with one detail from Cicero, that Archimedes' grave was not far out in the western countryside, but 'near' or 'towards' or 'against' the Achradina Gate ('ad portas Agragantinas'). It seems unlikely that he was simply shovelled under a pre-existing monument, since the fact that he was buried under a representation of a sphere and cylinder is the one detail we are fairly sure about. It is therefore possible, perhaps even plausible, that Archimedes was laid to rest among his ancestors, but under a custom-built marker that would have stood out as unique among the centuries-old monuments around it. Indeed, its uniqueness may have been one reason that, even in an overgrown state, Cicero was able to pick it out from among a 'great many tombs'.

So where is Archimedes now? In a sense, he is everywhere. His name can be found on the Archimedes Technopark on Viale Giuseppe Agnello, and the Centro Commerciale Archimede shopping mall on the Via per Canicattini roundabout, and on an oddly emaciated statue near Ponte Umbertino, holding what appears to be a radar dish but is probably intended to be one of his burning mirrors. He is in hotels too, from the Hotel Archimede Ortigia to the Dimora Archimedea north of town to the alleged grave in the courtyard of the Hotel Panorama, which is likely no more authentic than the one in the Archaeological Park. You can rent a room at Archimede Apartments in Ortygia, eat a meal at Il Cortile di

Archimede on via della Maestanza, or sip an espresso on Piazza
Archimede Caffè as you watch the waters play in the Fountain of
Diana.

Archimedes is arguably as ubiquitous a presence in modern
Siracusa as he ever was in the ancient city. Alas, he is not quite the
patron saint. That distinction still belongs to Santa Lucia, whose
massive teardrop-shaped sanctuary dominates the northern sky-
line. This makes a connection between the scientist and the martyr
almost too good a legend *not* to concoct. Dijksterhuis of all people
repeats an assertion published by David Rivault in the early seven-
teenth century, who in turn heard it from a 'learned Greek friend',
that the saint was a direct descendant of the great genius.[43] Even
if that were true, the five hundred years separating the death of
Archimedes from the birth of the martyr would make their blood
connection very tenuous indeed. So tenuous, in fact, that even if
we could sample the DNA of both Archimedes and St Lucia, modern
autosomal testing can detect only relationships going back some
five to seven generations – far short of five hundred years.[44]

But Archimedes is everywhere in Syracuse in another, less tangible sense. For the Romans who seized control of the history of
Syracuse and subsequently all of Sicily, the legacy of the genius was
as much part of the topography as the city's walls and markets. He
was killed, after all, while supposedly sketching in the very dirt
where his blood would soon be spilled ('and, slaughtered as dis-
regarding the victor's command, he disordered the outlines of his
own art with his own blood').[45] Robbed of the greatest prize of his
victory, Marcellus dutifully plants Archimedes in the same ground,
among his ancestors. But the grave is soon lost, and after a brief res-
toration by Cicero, is lost again. Much as the man himself neglected
his physical presence, Archimedes' mortal remains rapidly become
afterthoughts, existing both everywhere and nowhere in particular.

After immersing oneself in all things Archimedes, it is hard
to be satisfied with the faux grave in the Neapolis archaeological

zone. The former confines of the Fusco necropolis, meanwhile, are vast and intermittently built over. Starting in the general vicinity of the current municipal cemetery, I struck out along the shoulderless Viale Ermocrate, not knowing exactly what I was looking for. Perhaps I was hoping for some inkling, some kind of sympathetic vibration from the land that contained but obscured his final resting place.

To the right, the high ground of the Epipole plateau shimmered in the unseasonable heat. To the left, amber stripes of farmland were divided by power lines. The road was as ill-suited to pedestrians as a Los Angeles freeway, and I soon tired of dodging shredded tyres, dead cats and unwanted contact with heedless Sicilian drivers. Bathed in sweat, I trudged onwards, hoping to hear what I knew I wouldn't. After thirty more minutes of this, I came to accept the inescapable. If that sphere and cylinder ever saw the light of modern day, it might have been by some construction crew erecting a building or clearing a road, in the area west of the train station and north of the Centro Commerciale Archimede, and, for fear of meddling antiquarians and archaeologists, been quietly 'lost'. I caught a taxi back to the Piazza Archimede and consoled myself with a sweet cream gelato.

Pantheon

To the writer of this book and hopefully to those who have read it, the importance of Archimedes in the history of science is indisputable. And yet, even as he appears to be having a cultural 'moment', he fares poorly in lists of the greatest scientists in history. He does not appear at all on the list compiled by *Discover* magazine in 2023.[46] In a meta-list (a list of lists) posted in 2020, he ranks below Marie Curie, James Clerk Maxwell and Stephen Hawking, as well as figures who outright venerated him, including Galileo and Tesla.[47] The *Discover* list gives prominence to Pythagoras, Isaac Asimov and Bill Nye the Science Guy – individuals whose primary contributions arguably did not lie in *doing* science at all – and never mentions the Syracusan. Carl Sagan gets an honourable mention, but it is hard to imagine even the famously self-important Sagan placing himself in the same league as Archimedes.

Where does he really belong on such a list? It is hard to deny the primacy of giants responsible for the monumental paradigms, such as classical mechanics (Newton), biological evolution (Darwin and Alfred Russel Wallace) and relativity (Einstein). If we want to fill out the scale from the very smallest to the very biggest, the originators of quantum theory, such as Max Planck and Niels Bohr, also deserve a prominent place.

But for the reasons explored throughout this book, Archimedes is second to none among these epochal figures. Even when most of his output seemed lost, Archimedes' influence lay beneath the surface, inspiring descendants in both East and West through the sheer formidability of his reputation. Just as his defence of Syracuse defined how profoundly a single genius could influence great events, Archimedes stood for centuries as the archetype of what a solitary yet disciplined mind could accomplish. Where Newton saw himself as 'a child playing on the beach, while vast oceans of truth lie undiscovered before me', the mind of Archimedes shone like one of his apocryphal mirrors, casting a a hard light over a narrower but still obscure sea. History has yet to take the full measure of him.

REFERENCES

Prologue

1 Plutarch, *Life of Marcellus*, trans. B. Perrin (Cambridge, MA, 1923), Sec. 17.
2 Steven Strogatz, *Infinite Powers: How Calculus Reveals the Secrets of the Universe* (Boston, MA, and New York, 2019), pp. 27–57.

1 Engineer

1 Cicero, *Tusculan Disputations*, trans. C. Yonge (New York, 1877), v.23.
2 John Tzetzes, *Chiliades*, ed. T. Kiesslingius (Leipzig, 1826), trans. A. Untila et al., available at www.topostext.org, 2.102, accessed 14 November 2023.
3 Ibid., 2.140.
4 Justin, *Epitome of the Philippic History of Pompeius Trogus*, Corpus Scriptorum Latinorum, trans. J. Watson (London, 1853), 23.4, available at www.forumromanum.org, accessed 28 August 2023.
5 Nicholas Nicastro, *Circumference: Eratosthenes and the Ancient Quest to Measure the Globe* (New York, 2008), p. 75.
6 Diodorus Siculus, *Library of History*, trans. C. Oldfather (Cambridge, MA, 1933), 1.34.2 and 5.37.3–4.
7 S. Dalley and J. Oleson, 'Sennacherib, Archimedes, and the Water Screw: The Context of Invention in the Ancient World', *Technology and Culture*, XLIV/1 (2003), pp. 1–26 (p. 7).
8 Ibid., p. 25.
9 Cicero, *Tusculan Disputations*, v.23, and Silius Italicus, *Punica*, trans. J. Duff (Cambridge, MA, 1934), XIV, line 343.
10 See Netz, who wonders if a biography of Archimedes 'should not be attempted at all'. Reviel Netz, *The Works of Archimedes* (Cambridge, 2004), vol. I, p. 10.
11 Thucydides, *The Peloponnesian War*, trans. R. Crawley [1874] and ed. R. Strassler (New York, 1996), 6.3.
12 Ovid, *Metamorphoses*, trans. F. Miller (Cambridge, MA, 1951), Book v.
13 Though dwarf varieties of papyrus are native to Sicily, true Egyptian papyrus (*Cyperus papyrus*) was probably introduced in historical times, either by the Phoenicians, or directly from the Ptolemaic kingdom in the third century BCE.
14 Jeremy Dummett, *Syracuse, City of Legends: A Glory of Sicily* (London, 2010), p. 23.

15 Ibid., p. 7.
16 Ibid., p. 10.
17 Herodotus, *History*, trans. D. Grene (Chicago, IL, 1987), Book VII, 155.
18 Ibid., Book VII, 145.
19 Gelon's extravagant offer was never put to the test, as the tyrant demanded overall command of the Greek resistance to Xerxes, which the Spartans and Athenians would never accept.
20 Diodorus Siculus, *Library*, Book XI, 26.
21 Thucydides, *Peloponnesian War*, Book VII.
22 Werner Soedel and Vernard Foley, 'Ancient Catapults', *Scientific American*, CCXL/3 (1979), pp. 150–61.
23 Aristotle, *The Politics of Aristotle*, trans. B. Jowett (Oxford, 1885), XI 28, available at http://classics.mit.edu,. accessed 28 August 2023.
24 Silius Italicus, *Punica*, XIV.l.641–2.
25 Plutarch, 'Life of Dion, in *Lives*, trans. B. Perrin, vol. VI (Cambridge, MA, 1918), Sec. 7, available at LacusCurtius, https://penelope.uchicago.edu, accessed 28 August 2023.
26 Plato, *Seventh Letter*, trans. J. Harward, Internet Classics Archive, http://classics.mit.edu, accessed 28 August 2023. The authenticity of this source, one of his few surviving writings outside the dialogues, has lately been called into question (see, for example, M. Burnyeat and M. Frede, *The Pseudo-Platonic Seventh Letter*, ed. D. Scott (Oxford, 2015)). But many others still consider it an actual work of Plato (C. Kahn, 'The Pseudo-Platonic Seventh Letter', Notre Dame Philosophical Reviews, www.ndpr.nd.edu, 9 November 2015).
27 Plutarch, 'Life of Pyrrhus, in *Lives*, trans. B. Perrin, vol. IX (Cambridge, MA, 1920), Sec. 14, available at LacusCurtius, https://penelope.uchicago.edu, accessed 28 August 2023.
28 Cicero, *Against Verres*, trans. C. Yonge (London, 1903), Sec. 52–6.
29 Usman Aslam, 'How Many People Can a Cow Feed?', https://farmingbase. com, accessed 10 August 2023.
30 Livy, *History of Rome*, trans. C. Roberts (London, 1905), XXII.37, available at www.perseus.tufts.edu, accessed 14 November 2023.
31 Polybius, *Histories*, trans. E. S. Shuckburgh (London, 1889), I.83, available at www.perseus.tufts.edu, accessed 14 November 2023.
32 Andrew Lang, trans.,*Theocritus, Bion and Moschus: Rendered into English Prose* (London, 1880), Idyll XVI, available at www.gutenberg,org, accessed 28 August 2023.
33 See, for example, Giovanna De Sensi Sestito, who appears to cite a non-existent passage in Plutarch; see Giovanni di Pasquale, Claudio Parisi Presicce and Giovanna De Sensi Sestito, eds, *Archimedes: The Art and Science of Invention*, exh. cat., Musei Capitolini, Rome (2013), p. 28.
34 Plutarch, 'Life of Marcellus', *Lives*, in trans. B. Perrin (Cambridge, MA, 1917), vol. V, Sec. 14, available at LacusCurtius, https://penelope.uchicago.edu, accessed 28 August 2023.
35 Archimedes, *Method of Mechanical Theorems*, trans. T. Heath (Garden City, NY, 2002), dedication.
36 Proclus, *Proclus: A Commentary on the First Book of Euclid's Elements*, trans. G. Morrow (Princeton, NJ, 1992), p. 51.

37 John Tzetzes, *Chiliades*, 2. Doing a task 'with the left hand' can connote something that is almost casually easy, not even requiring the right hand. Or it can imply something distasteful, such as wiping oneself in the latrine.

38 Kevin Greene, 'Inventors, Invention, and Attitudes toward Technology and Innovation', in *The Oxford Handbook of Engineering and Technology in the Classical World*, ed. John Peter Oleson (Oxford, 2008), pp. 800–818 (p. 807).

39 Indeed, none of the biographical sketches in Plutarch's *Parallel Lives* are about any scientist or poet, or writer, or artist. To illustrate the eternal verities of character in history, Plutarch stuck to lawgivers, kings and generals.

40 Polybius, *Histories*, 8.5–7.

41 Paul T. Keyser, 'The Archimedean 'sambukē' of Damis in Biton', *Archive for History of Exact Sciences*, LXXVI (2022), pp. 153–72.

42 Demonstrated to the author at Archimedes Technopark, Siracusa, Italy, June 2022.

43 Polybius, *Histories*, 8.3.2; Livy, *History of Rome*, 24.34.4.

44 Chris Rorres and Harry G. Harris, 'A Formidable War Machine: Construction and Operation of Archimedes' Iron Hand', available at www.researchgate.net, accessed 8 December 2023. The authors assume Archimedes would have placed one machine to cover a length of wall equal to one Roman quinquereme, or about 36 metres.

45 C. K. Young, 'Archimedes's Iron Hand or Claw: A New Interpretation of an Old Mystery', *Centaurus*, XLVI (2004), pp. 189–207 (p. 193).

46 Ibid.

47 Plutarch, 'Life of Marcellus', 17.3.

48 Polybius, *Histories*, 8.6.

49 Plutarch, 'Life of Marcellus', 17.

50 Polybius, *Histories*, 8.3.

51 U.S. Marine Corps/Army Techniques Publication (ATP) 3-09.42, Fire Support for the Brigade Combat Team.

52 Plutarch, 'Life of Marcellus', 17.

53 Livy, *History of Rome*, XXV.31.

54 Ibid.

55 Plutarch, 'Life of Marcellus', 19.

56 Eduard Jan Dijksterhuis, *Archimedes* (Princeton, NJ, 1938), p. 31.

57 Tzetzes, *Chiliades*, 2.

58 Ioannes Zonaras, *Epitome of the Lost Books I–XXI of Dio*, in H. B. Foster, *Dio's Annals of Rome*, vol. I (New York, 1905), p. 241.

59 Cettina Voza, 'The Death of Archimedes: A Reassessment', in *The Genius of Archimedes: 23 Centuries of Influence on Mathematics, Science and Engineering*, ed. Stephanos A. Paipetis and Marco Ceccarelli (Dordrecht, 2010), pp. 507–13.

60 Ibid., p. 511.

61 Dijksterhuis, *Archimedes*, pp. 31–2.

62 Plutarch, 'Life of Marcellus', 19.

63 John Tzetzes, however, says 'the killer of Archimedes, I think, Marcellus kills with an axe'. Tzetzes, *Chiliades*, 2.

64 Ibid.

65 Plutarch, 'Life of Marcellus', 17.

66 Cicero, *Tusculan Disputations*, v.23.
67 Dennis L. Simms, 'The Trail for Archimedes' Tomb', *Journal of the Warburg and Courtauld Institutes*, LIII (1990), pp. 281–6 (p. 284).
68 Plutarch, 'Life of Marcellus', 14.
69 Marshall Clagett, *The Science of Mechanics in the Middle Ages* (Madison, WI, 1959), pp. 24–30.
70 Another way to say this is that two 2-kilogram weights can replace a single 4-kilogram weight on the end of a lever and it will balance exactly the same. The sole condition is that the centre of gravity of the two former weights is the same as the latter, lying at the same distance from the fulcrum.
71 Thomas Heath, *The Works of Archimedes* (Cambridge, 1897; repr. Garden City, NY, 2002), p. vi.
72 Dennis L. Simms, 'Archimedes and the Burning Mirrors of Syracuse', *Technology and Culture*, XVIII/1 (1977), pp. 1–24 (p. 7).
73 Tzetzes, *Chiliades*, 2.
74 Zonaras, *Epitome*, p. 239.
75 Simms, 'Archimedes and the Burning Mirrors', p. 18.
76 W. E. Knowles Middleton, 'Archimedes, Kircher, Buffon, and the Burning-Mirrors', *Isis*, LII/4 (1961), pp. 533–43 (p. 539).
77 The MythBusters' attempt did demonstrate one interesting fact: while it is common to assume that sails would be easier to ignite than wood, it was actually harder because sails move in the wind, changing shape and position. This movement dissipates thermal energy at the focal point of the mirrors. So if the Romans somehow did approach under full sail (which they wouldn't), their sails would not have been practical targets for burning either.
78 Apuleius, *Apologia*, in *The Apologia and Florida of Apuleius of Madauira*, trans. H. E. Butler (Oxford, 1909), 1.16, available as 'The Defense' at Internet Classics Archive, http://classics.mit.edu, accessed 15 November 2023. *Contra* Plutarch, this is another Archimedean treatise on a practical subject.
79 Martin Wallraff et al., eds, *Iulius Africanus: Cesti: The Extant Fragments* (Berlin and Boston, MA, 2012), D25, pp. 116–17.
80 Simms, 'Archimedes and the Burning Mirrors', p. 24.
81 Vitruvius, *De Architectura*, trans. M. Morgan (New York, 1960), Book IX, 9–12. A short version of the story appears a century later in Plutarch's essay 'That Epicurus Actually Makes a Pleasant Life Impossible', *Plutarch's Moralia*, trans. B. Einarson and P. H. De Lacey (Cambridge, MA, and London, 1959), vol. XIV, 1094 C, p. 67, available at https://archive.org, accessed 15 November 2023.
82 Reviel Netz and William Noel, *The Archimedes Codex* (London, 2008), p. 53.
83 Quintilian, *Institutio oratoria*, trans. H. E. Butler (Cambridge, MA, 1920), 12.10.9; Plutarch, 'Life of Pericles', in *Lives*, trans. B. Perrin, vol. III (Cambridge, MA, 1916), Sec. 31, available at LacusCurtius, https://penelope.uchicago.edu, accessed 28 August 2023.
84 Ronald S. Stroud, 'An Athenian Law on Silver Coinage', *Hesperia*, XLIII/2 (1974), pp. 157–88.
85 Bolos of Mendes, *Physika*, quoted in *Greek Science of the Hellenistic Era: A Sourcebook*, ed. Georgia Irby-Massie and Paul T. Keyser (London, 2002), p. 236.
86 For example, Mary Jaeger, *Archimedes and the Roman Imagination* (Ann Arbor, MI, 2013), p. 17.

87 Cicero, *On Divination*, trans. W. A. Falconer (Cambridge, MA, 1923), 22.37, 1.24, available at LacusCurtius, www.penelope.uchicago.edu, accessed 28 August 2023.

88 For example, Reviel Netz, *Ludic Proof: Greek Mathematics and the Alexandrian Aesthetic* (Cambridge, 2021).

89 Favinus, *Carmen de ponderibus et mensuris*, in *Prisciani Grammatici de laude Imperatoris Anastasii et de Ponderibus et mensuris carmina*, ed. S. L. Endlicher (Vienna, 1828), lines 124–62, pp. 93–4, available at www.archive. org, accessed 28 August 2023.

90 Alan Hirshfeld, *Eureka Man: The Life and Legacy of Archimedes* (New York, 2009), pp. 75–7.

91 Irby-Massie and Keyser, *Greek Science of the Hellenistic Era*, p. 205.

92 Dijksterhuis, *Archimedes*, pp. 48–9.

93 Athenaeus, *Deipnosophistae*, trans. C. Gulick (Cambridge, MA, 1941), 5:40; Plutarch, 'Life of Marcellus', 14.

94 Reviel Netz, *A New History of Greek Mathematics* (Cambridge, 2022), pp. 137–8.

95 Jean MacIntosh Turfa and Alwin G. Steinmayer Jr, 'The *Syracusia* as a Giant Cargo Vessel', *International Journal of Nautical Archaeology*, XXVIII/2 (1999), pp. 105–25 (p. 118).

96 Lucian, *Navigium*, 5, in *The Works of Lucian of Samosata*, trans. H. W. Fowler and F. G. Fowler (Oxford, 1905), available at https:// lucianofsamosata.info, accessed 15 November 2023.

97 Turfa and Steinmayer, 'The *Syracusia* as a Giant Cargo Vessel', p. 117. About 1,000 crew are listed by Athenaeus. Adding oarsmen and so forth, Turfa and Steinmayer estimate a likely complement of almost 2,000. U.S. Navy *Iowa*-class battleships carried a crew of 1,800 by the end of their operational lives in the 1980s; ibid., pp. 118–25.

98 Athenaeus, *Deipnosophistae*, 5:206d–209b.

99 Plutarch, 'Life of Demetrius', in *Lives*, trans. H. E. Butler, vol. IX (Cambridge, MA, 1920), 43:4.

100 For example, Jo Marchant, *Decoding the Heavens* (Cambridge, MA, 2009) and Alexander Jones, *A Portable Cosmos* (Oxford, 2017).

101 T. Freeth et al., 'A Model of the Cosmos in the Ancient Greek Antikythera Mechanism', *Scientific Reports*, , www.nature.com, 12 March 2021; M. T. Wright and A. G. Bromley, 'Towards a New Reconstruction of the Antikythera Mechanism', in *Extraordinary Machines and Structures in Antiquity*, ed. S. A. Paipetis (Patras, 2003), pp. 81–94.

102 Ed Grabianowski, 'Advanced Imaging Reveals a Computer 1,500 Years Ahead of Its Time', www.gizmodo.com, 8 January 2010.

103 Marchant, *Decoding the Heavens*, p. 288.

104 Nicastro, *Circumference*, pp. 75–6.

105 Marchant, *Decoding the Heavens*, p. 286.

106 Herbert Bruderer, 'The Antikythera Mechanism', *Communications of the* ACM [Association for Computing Machinery], LXIII/4 (April 2020), pp. 108–15.

107 Tony Freeth, 'An Ancient Greek Astronomical Calculation Machine Reveals New Secrets', *Scientific American*, www.scientificamerican.com, 1 January 2022.

108 Marchant, *Decoding the Heavens*, p. 244.

109 Dijksterhuis, *Archimedes*, p. 25.

110 Pappus, *Collection*, ed. F. O. Hultsch, vol. III (Berlin, 1878), Book VIII.25, Latin trans., available at www.archive.org, accessed 15 November 2023.

111 Ovid, *Ovid's Fasti*, trans. Sir James George Frazer (Cambridge, MA, 1933), Book VI, lines 276–8, available at www.perseus.tufts.edu, accessed 28 August 2023.

112 Cicero, *De Republica*, trans. C. Keyes (Cambridge, MA, 1928), 1.14. If we had taken Cicero at his word from the beginning, the discovery of such a complex instrument as the Antikythera Mechanism would not have come as a surprise.

113 For example, Cicero, *Tusculan Disputations*, 1.34.

114 Cicero, *On the Nature of the Gods*, trans. F. Brooks (London, 1896), 2.34–5.

115 Bruderer, 'The Antikythera Mechanism', pp. 108–15.

116 Netz, *A New History of Greek Mathematics*, pp. 177–9.

117 The device was called the πιθήκιον, or 'little ape'. Athenaeus Mechanicus, *On Machines*, IV.1. In D. Whitehead and P. H. Blyth, *Athenaeus Mechanicus, Peri mēchanēmatōn*, Historia Einzelschriften 182 (Stuttgart, 2004), p. 101.

118 There are fascinating reconstructions of many of Heron's devices at the Kotsanas Museum in Athens.

119 Pliny, *Natural History*, trans. J. Healy (New York, 1991), 2.117.

120 Moses I. Finley, *The Ancient Economy* (Berkeley, CA, 1973).

121 Kevin Green, 'Technological Innovation and Economic Progress in the Ancient World: M. I. Finley Re-Considered', *Economic History Review*, LIII/1 (February 2000), pp. 29–59.

122 Peter Green, *Alexander to Actium: The Historical Evolution of the Hellenistic Age* (Berkeley, CA, 1993), p. 472. Green otherwise accepts Plutarch's image of an 'oblivious', practically impractical Archimedes.

123 Seneca, *Moral Letters*, trans. R. Gummere (Cambridge, MA, 1917–25), 90.15, available at https//topostext.org, accessed 15 November 2023.

124 Ibid., 90.30.

125 Tacitus, *Annals of Imperial Rome*, trans. M. Grant (New York, 1993), pp. 304–5.

126 Epicurus, *Letter to Pythocles*, in *Epicurus: The Extant Remains*, trans. C. Bailey (Oxford, 1926), 85.

127 Netz, *A New History of Greek Mathematics*, pp. 126–7.

128 For example, Charles Freeman, *The Closing of the Western Mind* (New York, 2005).

129 Marshall Clagett, *Greek Science in Antiquity* (New York, 1963), p. 15.

130 Jaeger, *Archimedes and the Roman Imagination*, p. 47.

131 Netz, *A New History of Greek Mathematics*, pp. 53–6.

132 Indeed, contemporary claims that he personally built the Antikythera Mechanism suggest that his legend as engineer is still growing.

2 Mathematician

1 L. D. Reynolds and N. G. Wilson, *Scribes and Scholars: A Guide to the Transmission of Greek and Latin Literature*, 4th edn (Oxford, 2013), pp. 2–5.

2 Reviel Netz and William Noel, *The Archimedes Codex* (London, 2008), p. 108.

3 Diocles, *On Burning Mirrors*, trans. G. Toomer (Berlin, 1975), 1.2, 34, 36, 42, 140.

4 Theon, *Commentary on Ptolemy's Almagest*, trans. A. Rome (Rome, 1931), 1.3.

5 Thomas Heath, *The Works of Archimedes* (Cambridge, 1897; repr. Garden City, NY, 2002), p. xxxv.

6 Eduard Jan Dijksterhuis, *Archimedes* (Princeton, NJ, 1938), pp. 34–5.
7 Netz and Noel, *The Archimedes Codex*, p. 47.
8 Reviel Netz, *The Works of Archimedes* (Cambridge, 2004), pp. 20, 25.
9 Luciano Canfora, *The Vanished Library* (Berkeley, CA, 1990), p. 87.
10 Martial, *Epigrams* (London, 1897), 1.2, rev. at www.tertullian.org, accessed 30 August 2023.
11 Ibid., 14.190.
12 T. C. Skeat, 'The Length of the Standard Papyrus Roll and the Cost-Advantage of the Codex', *Zeitschrift für Papyrologie und Epigraphik*, XLV (1982), pp. 169–75.
13 Colin H. Roberts and T. C. Skeat, *The Birth of the Codex* (London, 1987), p. 1.
14 Kim Haines-Eitzen, 'Codex', in *The Encyclopedia of Ancient History*, ed. A. Erskine et al. (Chichester, 2013), p. 1595.
15 Interestingly, texts like Archimedes' actually benefited from random access, as anyone obliged to flip back and forth to the illustrations to follow a geometrical argument will attest.
16 Netz and Noel, *The Archimedes Codex*, p. 81.
17 See Jim Al-Khalili, *The House of Wisdom: How Arabic Science Saved Ancient Knowledge and Gave Us the Renaissance* (London, 2010) for extended discussion.
18 Heath, *The Works of Archimedes*, p. xxxii.
19 Ibid., p. 221.
20 B. L. Van der Waerden, *Science Awakening*, trans. A. Dresden (New York, 1961), pp. 45–7.
21 Ibid.
22 Archimedes, *Sand-Reckoner*, in Heath, *The Works of Archimedes*, p. 223.
23 Ibid., p. 222.
24 Steven Strogatz, *Infinite Powers: How Calculus Reveals the Secrets of the Universe* (Boston, MA, and New York, 2019), pp. 31–2.
25 'What Are Kalpas?', www.lionsroar.com, 14 December 2016.
26 Netz and Noel, *The Archimedes Codex*, p. 287.
27 Indeed, in his *New History of Greek Mathematics* (Cambridge, 2022), Reviel Netz confidently asserts a scholarly consensus that '*Pythagoras did no mathematics whatsoever*' (emphasis in original), p. 17.
28 Cicero, *Tusculan Disputations*, trans. C. Yonge (New York, 1877), 5.3.8–9.
29 Aristotle, *Metaphysics*, trans. W. Ross (Oxford, 1924), Book 1, part v.
30 Iamblichus, *Life of Pythagoras*, trans. T. Taylor (London, 1818), chap. xxxiv, p. 126.
31 K. D. White, '"The Base Mechanic Arts"? Some Thoughts on the Contribution of Science (Pure and Applied) to the Culture of the Hellenistic Age', in *Hellenistic History and Culture*, ed. Peter Green (Berkeley, CA, 1993), p. 237.
32 Strogatz, *Infinite Powers*, p. 33.
33 Indeed, the conceptual gap between the Greeks' geometrical and the algebraic shorthand we define as 'modern' isn't just a matter of historical interest. Though I got high grades in my own mathematical education, earning advanced placement in college courses when I graduated from high school, manipulating algebraic symbols alone never came easily. Some kind of concrete visualization was always helpful. And indeed, virtually all maths instruction (and virtually all scholarly and popular publications on the

subject, including ones consulted in writing this book) use illustrations – whether they be plots or geometric figures – to exemplify difficult concepts. In this sense, we are still all like the ancient Greeks, preferring to ground our shorthand in things we can visualize.

34 Liu Dun, 'A Comparison of Archimedes' and Liu Hiu's Studies of Circles', *Journal of Dialectics of Nature*, vii/1 (1985), pp. 51–60.

35 Indeed, it is easy to imagine a purely pragmatic tradition achieving an excellent estimate of π by laying out very large circles on a flat piece of land and measuring their diameters and circumferences very precisely. At Tell al-Amarna, the ancient Egyptians achieved better than 99.641 per cent accuracy laying out boundary markers as long as 15 kilometres. Such a 'geodetic' approach, if done at a similar level of scale and accuracy, would likely have resulted in values for π running into multiple decimal places. But philosophically inclined Greeks would have scorned such approaches.

36 1 Kings 7:23–6.

37 Otto Neugebauer, *The Exact Sciences in Antiquity* (New York, 1969), pp. 46–8.

38 Heath, *The Works of Archimedes*, pp. 91–8.

39 Netz, *A New History of Greek Mathematics*, p. 158.

40 Matthew Humphries, 'Google Cloud Sets World Record by Calculating Pi to 100 Trillion Digits', *PCMag*, www.pcmag.com, 9 June 2022.

41 Dijksterhuis, *Archimedes*, pp. 56–7; Nicholas Nicastro, *Circumference: Eratosthenes and the Ancient Quest to Measure the Globe* (New York, 2008), pp. 90–95.

42 Wyatte C. Hooper, 'Archimedes of Syracuse and Sir Isaac Newton: On the Quadrature of a Parabola', *Journal of Humanistic Mathematics*, xi/2 (2021), pp. 374–91 (p. 376).

43 Neil deGrasse Tyson [@neiltyson], 'Math is the language of the universe. So the more equations you know, the more you can converse with the cosmos', https://twitter.com, 21 November 2021.

44 Heath, *The Works of Archimedes*, p. 13 (addendum).

45 Suda On Line, www.stoa.org, θ 142.

46 Hermann Schöne, *Heronis Alexandrini Opera* (Leipzig, 1903), vol. iii, pp. 80, line 17; 130, line 15; and 130, line 25.

47 Andre Koch Torres Assis and Ceno Pietro Magnaghi, *The Illustrated Method of Archimedes* (Montreal, 2012), pp. 27–36.

48 Euclid, *Elements*, trans. T. L. Heath (Cambridge, 1908), Book xii, Prop. 2, available at www.perseus.tufts.edu, accessed 16 November 2023.

49 Ibid., Book xii, Prop. 10.

50 Claude Lévi-Strauss, *The Savage Mind* (London, 1966), pp. 16–22 (emphasis added).

51 H. Hankel, *Zur Geschichte der Mathematik im Altertum und Mittelalter* (Leipzig, 1874), p. 164, trans. in Ulrich Lirecht, *Chinese Mathematics in the Thirteenth Century* (New York, 1973), pp. 218–19.

52 Carl B. Boyer, *A History of Mathematics* (New York, 1991), p. 22.

53 Al-Khalili, *The House of Wisdom*, pp. 110–23.

54 Lévi-Strauss, *The Savage Mind*, p. 18.

55 Giangiacomo Martines, 'The Conception and Construction of Drum and Dome', in *The Pantheon: From Antiquity to the Present*, ed. Tod A. Marder and Mark Wilson Jones (Cambridge, 2015), pp. 130–31.

56 Eli Maor, *To Infinity and Beyond: A Cultural History of the Infinite* (Princeton, NJ, 1987), pp. 2–9.

57 Modern 'Set Theory' does posit the concept of a 'countable' sort of infinity, as long as some number can conceivably be assigned to every member of an infinite set. But this notion would likely have flummoxed the Greeks as thoroughly as it did those modern critics who drove its originator, Georg Cantor (1845–1918), to despair in his lifetime.

58 Aristotle, *Physics*, Book III, Chapter 7.

59 Heath, *The Works of Archimedes*, p. 17 (addendum).

60 Strogatz, *Infinite Powers*, pp. 169–72.

61 Heath, *The Works of Archimedes*, pp. 238–43.

62 Ibid., p. 14 (addendum).

63 Archimedes, *On the Sphere and Cylinder*, Book I, dedication; see Heath, *The Works of Archimedes*, p. 2.

64 Wilbur R. Knorr, *The Ancient Tradition of Geometric Problems* (New York, 1993), p. 79 (emphasis added).

65 Aristotle, *Metaphysics*, 12.8.

3 Legacy

1 Marshall Clagett, *Archimedes in the Middle Ages* (Madison, WI, 1964), pp. 1–14.

2 Marc Cenedella, 'Even a Genius Has to Sell Himself . . . The Remarkable Resume of Leonardo da Vinci', https://rooting-for-you.cenedella.com, accessed 16 November 2023.

3 D. L. Simms, 'Archimedes' Weapons of War and Leonardo', *British Journal for the History of Science*, XXI/2 (June 1988), pp. 195–210 (p. 205).

4 Ibid., pp. 195–6.

5 A 1:5 scale model was successfully tested by the Greek engineer Ioannis Sakas in the 1980s. Ibid., p. 198.

6 Speech by Demetrius Chalcondyles at the University of Padua, 1463, in Deno John Geanakoplos, ed., *Byzantium: Church, Society, and Civilization Seen through Contemporary Eyes* (Chicago, IL, 1984), p. 444.

7 Letter to Kepler, 19 August 1610, in Karl von Gebler, *Galileo Galilei and the Roman Curia* (London, 1879), p. 26.

8 Ibid.

9 Galileo, *Dialogue Concerning the Two Chief World Systems* (Berkeley, CA, 1967), p. 289.

10 For example, Thony Christie, 'Galileo's Reputation Is More Hyperbole than Truth', *Aeon*, www.aeon.co, 31 March 2016.

11 Isaac Newton, *Principia*, Prop. LXXIX, Theorem XXXIX, available at https://cudl.lib.cam.ac.uk, accessed 31 August 2023.

12 For example, Alan Hirshfeld, *Eureka Man: The Life and Legacy of Archimedes* (New York, 2009), p. 176.

13 For example, Jeff Powers, 'Did Archimedes Do Calculus?', https://maa.org, 30 March 2020.

14 Thomas Heath, *The Works of Archimedes* (Cambridge, 1897; repr. Garden City, NY, 2002), p. cliii.

15 Peter Ackroyd, *Newton* (London, 2008), p. 78.

ARCHIMEDES

16 Ibid., pp. 29–30.
17 Marianne Bergmann, 'The Philosophers and Poets in the Sarapieion at Memphis', in *Early Hellenistic Portraiture*, ed. P. Schultz and R. Von den Hoff (Cambridge, 2007), pp. 246–64 (p. 259).
18 Ibid., p. 261.
19 Diodorus Siculus, *Library of History*, trans. C. Oldfather (Cambridge, MA, 1933), 1.96.
20 Bergmann, 'The Philosophers and Poets in the Sarapieion at Memphis', p. 255.
21 Gisela M. A. Richter, *The Portraits of the Greeks* (Ithaca, NY, 1984), p. 120.
22 Heath, *The Works of Archimedes*, pp. 1–2.
23 Cassius Dio, *Roman History*, trans. E. Cary, vol. VI (Cambridge, MA, 1917), LIII.27, available at www.lexundria.com, accessed 31 August 2023. Writing in Greek, he actually makes reference to Ares and Aphrodite, but the translator substitutes the Roman counterparts.
24 Nicomachus, *Introduction to Arithmetic*, trans. M. D'Ooge (New York, 1926), Book 1, chap. 16.
25 There are various figures for the length of the lunar month, depending on how it is measured. The number of days for the Moon to complete a full cycle of phases (the 'synodic' month) is 29.53 days. But the Moon returns to the same point in the sky, as seen against background stars (the 'sidereal' month) every 27.32 days. There is a difference because the Earth is also moving through space – a fact not accepted by most ancients.
26 David M. Jacobson, 'Hadrianic Architecture and Geometry', *American Journal of Archaeology*, XC/1 (January 1986), pp. 69–85.
27 Cassius Dio, *Roman History*, LXIX.4.
28 W.-D. Heilmeyer, 'Apollodorus von Damaskus, der Architekt des Pantheon', *Jahrbuch des Deutschen Archäologischen Instituts*, XC (1975), pp. 316–47.
29 Licinia Alberti and Miguel Ángel Alonso-Rodríguez, 'Geometrical Analysis of the Coffers of the Pantheon's Dome in Rome', *Nexus Network Journal*, XIX/2 (2017), pp. 363–82.
30 Giangiacomo Martines, 'Argomenti di geometria antica a proposito della cupola del Pantheon', *Quaderni dell'istituto di storia dell'architettura*, 13 (1989), pp. 3–10 (pp. 4–5).
31 Summarized in Alberti and Alonso-Rodríguez, 'Geometrical Analysis', p. 368.
32 Ibid., p. 369.
33 Cicero, *Tusculan Disputations*, trans. C. Yonge (New York, 1877), 1.2.
34 Procopius, *De Aedificiis*, trans. in W. Lethaby and H. Swainson, *The Church of Sancta Sophia Constantinople: A Study in Byzantine Building* (New York, 1894), pp. 24–8.
35 Paul the Silentiary, ibid., pp. 42–52.
36 Agathias, *Historia*, trans. J. Frendo (Berlin, 1979), Book 5, chaps 6–7.
37 Silius Italicus, *Punica*, 14.676–8, trans. in Mary Jaeger, *Archimedes and the Roman Imagination* (Ann Arbor, MI, 2013), p. 94.
38 Jaeger, *Archimedes and the Roman Imagination*, pp. 93–100.
39 Martial, *Epigrams* (London, 1897), 11.48, rev. at www.tertullian.org, accessed 30 August 2023.
40 Ibid., 11.49.
41 D. Mertens and H. Beste, 'Archimedes and the City Walls of Syracuse', in *Archimedes: The Art and Science of Invention*, ed. Giovanni di Pasquale,

182

Claudio Parisi Presicce and Giovanna De Sensi Sestito, exh. cat., Musei
   Capitolini, Rome (2013), p. 39.
42 Paolo Orsi, *Gli scavi nella necropoli del Fusco a Siracusa* (Rome, 1895).
43 Eduard Jan Dijksterhuis, *Archimedes* (Princeton, NJ, 1938), p. 11.
44 Diahan Southard, 'Limits of DNA Testing for Family History',
   www.yourdnaguide.com, accessed 17 December 2022.
45 Valerius Maximus, *Factorum et dictorum memorabilium libri IX*, 8.7.ext. 7;
   quoted in Jaeger, *Archimedes and the Roman Imagination*, p. 77.
46 G. Tarlach et al., '10 Famous Scientists and Their Contributions', *Discover*,
   www.discovermagazine.com, 19 October 2023.
47 'The Greatest Scientists of All Time', *Make Lists, Not War: The Meta-Lists
   Website*, www.beckchris.com, accessed 23 December 2022.

SUGGESTED READING

Primary Sources

Archimedes, *Method of Mechanical Theorems*, trans. Thomas Heath (Garden City, NY, 2002)
——, *Sand-Reckoner*, trans. Thomas Heath (Garden City, NY, 2002)
Cicero, *Against Verres*, trans. C. Yonge (London, 1903)
——, *De Republica*, trans. C. Keyes (Cambridge, MA, 1928)
——, *Tusculan Disputations*, trans. C. Yonge (New York, 1877)
Livy, *History of Rome*, trans. C. Roberts (London, 1905), available at www.perseus.tufts.edu, accessed 14 November 2023
Plato, *Seventh Letter*, trans. J. Harward, Internet Classics Archive, http://classics.mit.edu, accessed 28 August 2023
Pliny, *Natural History*, trans. J. Healy (New York, 1991)
Plutarch, *Life of Marcellus*, trans. B. Perrin (Cambridge, MA, 1923)
Polybius, *Histories*, trans. E. S. Shuckburgh (London, 1889), available at www.perseus.tufts.edu, accessed 14 November 2023
Silius Italicus, *Punica*, trans. J. Duff (Cambridge, MA, 1934)
Tzetzes, John, *Chiliades*, ed. T. Kiesslingius (Leipzig, 1826), trans. A. Untila et al., available at www.topostext.org, accessed 14 November 2023

Secondary Sources

Al-Khilili, Jim, *The House of Wisdom: How Arabic Science Saved Ancient Knowledge and Gave Us the Renaissance* (London, 2010)
Assis, Andre Koch Torres, and Ceno Pietro Magnaghi, *The Illustrated Method of Archimedes* (Montreal, 2012)
Clagett, Marshall, *Greek Science in Antiquity* (New York, 1963)
——, *The Science of Mechanics in the Middle Ages* (Madison, WI, 1959)
Eduard, Jan Dijksterhuis, *Archimedes* (Princeton, NJ, 1938)
Dummett, Jeremy, *Syracuse, City of Legends: A Glory of Sicily* (London, 2010)
Freeman, Charles, *The Closing of the Western Mind* (New York, 2005)
Freeth, Tony, 'An Ancient Greek Astronomical Calculation Machine Reveals New Secrets', *Scientific American*, www.scientificamerican.com, 1 January 2022
——, et al., 'A Model of the Cosmos in the Ancient Greek Antikythera Mechanism', *Scientific Reports*, www.nature.com, 12 March 2021

Green, Peter, *Alexander to Actium: The Historical Evolution of the Hellenistic Age* (Berkeley, CA, 1993)

Heath, Thomas, *The Works of Archimedes* (Cambridge, 1897; repr. Garden City, NY, 2002)

Irby-Massie, Georgia, and Paul T. Keyser, eds, *Greek Science of the Hellenistic Era: A Sourcebook* (London, 2002)

Jaeger, Mary, *Archimedes and the Roman Imagination* (Ann Arbor, MI, 2013)

Knorr, Wilbur R., *The Ancient Tradition of Geometric Problems* (New York, 1993)

Lloyd, Geoffrey E. R., *Greek Science after Aristotle* (New York, 1973)

Marchant, Jo, *Decoding the Heavens* (Cambridge, MA, 2009)

Marder, Tod A., and Mark Wilson Jones, eds, *The Pantheon: From Antiquity to the Present* (Cambridge, 2015)

Netz, Reviel, *Ludic Proof* (Cambridge, 2021)

——, *A New History of Greek Mathematics* (Cambridge, 2022)

——, *The Works of Archimedes* (Cambridge, 2004)

——, and William Noel, *The Archimedes Codex* (London, 2008)

Neugebauer, Otto, *The Exact Sciences in Antiquity* (New York, 1969)

Nicastro, Nicholas, *Circumference: Eratosthenes and the Ancient Quest to Measure the Globe* (New York, 2008)

Norwich, John Julius, *Sicily: An Island at the Crossroads of History* (New York, 2015)

Reynolds, L. D., and N. G. Wilson, *Scribes and Scholars: A Guide to the Transmission of Greek and Latin Literature*, 4th edn (Oxford, 2013)

Roberts, Colin H., and T. C. Skeat, *The Birth of the Codex* (London, 1987)

Simms, Dennis L., 'The Trail for Archimedes' Tomb', *Journal of the Warburg and Courtauld Institutes*, LIII (1990), pp. 281–6

Soedel, Werner, and Vernard Foley, 'Ancient Catapults', *Scientific American*, CCXL/3 (1979), pp. 150–61

Strogatz, Steven, *Infinite Powers: How Calculus Reveals the Secrets of the Universe* (Boston, MA, and New York, 2019)

PHOTO ACKNOWLEDGEMENTS

The author and publishers wish to express their thanks to the sources listed below for illustrative material and/or permission to reproduce it. Some locations of artworks are also given below, in the interest of brevity:

Bibliothèque de l'Institut de France, Paris (MS 2173 (Manuscript B), fol. 33r): 27; photo courtesy Andrew Chugg: 28; diagrams redrawn: 6, 7, 8, 10 (after T. H. Heath, *The Works of Archimedes* [1897] (2002 edn)), 14 (after Steve Strogatz, *Infinite Powers: How Calculus Reveals the Secrets of the Universe* (Boston and New York, 2019)), 15, 16, 18 (after Wyatte C. Hooper, 'Archimedes of Syracuse and Sir Isaac Newton: On the Quadrature of a Parabola', *Journal of Humanistic Mathematics*, XI/2 (July 2021)), 19 (after Steve Strogatz, *Infinite Powers: How Calculus Reveals the Secrets of the Universe* (Boston, MA, and New York, 2019)), 20 (after T. H. Heath, *The Works of Archimedes* [1897] (2002 edn)), 21, 22–6 (after A.K.T. Assis and C. D. Magnaghi, *Illustrated Method of Archimedes* (Montreal, 2012), 29, 30, 31 (after G. Martines, 'Argomenti di Geometria Antica a Proposito della Cupola del Pantheon', *Quaderni dell' Instituto di Storia dell'Architettura Nova Serie*, Fasciolo 13 (Rome, 1989), pp. 3–10); photos Nicholas Nicastro: 9, 12; Pushkin Museum of Fine Arts, Moscow: 1; Schloss Sanssouci, Potsdam: 2; Städtische Galerie Liebieghaus, Frankfurt am Main: 5; from B. L. van der Waerden, *Erwachende Wissenschaft: Ägyptische, babylonische und griechische Mathematik* (Basel and Stuttgart, 1956): 13; Wikimedia Commons: 11 (photo Zde, CC BY-SA 4.0 International), 17 (photo Carole Raddato, CC BY-SA 2.0 Generic).

INDEX

Illustration numbers are indicated by *italics*